Dreaming Yourself Aware

Achieve your potential by understanding your dreams

Lots of exercises and free downloadable worksheets

Dr Joan Harthan

Skills Training Course
www.UoLearn.com

Dreaming yourself aware.

Find dream meanings and interpretations to understand what your dream means.
A dream book to become your own dream interpreter.
Use dreaming for goal setting to make life changes.

Lots of exercises and free downloadable worksheets.

Published by: Universe of Learning Ltd, reg number 6485477, Lancashire, UK
www.UoLearn.com, support@UoLearn.com

ISBN 978-1-84937-055-4

Other editions: ebook pdf format 978-1-84937-060-8
ebook epub format 978-1-84937-061-5

Praise for Dreaming Yourself Aware

"I found that it was a good exercise to open up my creativity. It will benefit my counselling skills and confidence in risk taking."

"It has been fun, interesting and helpful to find out about myself and help others in their search for themselves. It's changed my life."

"This is a masterpiece amongst self-help books. The insights I gained about myself, through understanding my dreams, have been truly amazing."

"This book led me, step by step, to discover things about myself that I previously had no idea about. It's changed my life."

"I was going through a difficult time when I read this book. I was able to use what I learned to make my life better. Thank you."

"If you go through the exercises in this book, and work on your dreams in the ways suggested, you can't fail but find something out about yourself that will amaze you."

"Dream, Analyse, Action – a recipe for success."

"This book will show you the difference dreams can make. It takes the reader by the hand and leads them into ever revolving doors of ways of working with their dreams, understanding them, and learning and growing through them."

"This book will show you how to approach your dreams creatively and think about them differently. What is mind-blowing is that these different ways of working with dreams keep coming! All clearly explained and accessible. So no matter where you are in your relationship with dreams, you can pick up this book and find a new perspective from a very experienced guide."

3

About the author: Dr Joan Harthan

Originally from Saddleworth (NE of Manchester) Joan currently lives in the East Midlands. She describes herself as a bridge between two camps. Having worked in mainstream academia for many years she acknowledges the spiritual aspect of dreaming and has a particular interest in Shamanic dream work.

Her successful and varied career, developed relatively late in life, was directed and informed by her dreams. Following many years of living in the grey twilight of what if, may be, when and if, her dreams encouraged her to make the decision to go to University at age 37. She graduated with a PhD in Chemistry and took up a Teaching Fellowship at The University of Nottingham. Four years later she moved into the FE sector where she was employed as a Lecturer in Clinical Physiology / Biomedical Science before returning to The University of Nottingham as a Lecturer in Food Science. Here she instigated undergraduate research into the dreams of women attending a bone density clinic to see whether deteriorating bone condition was being reflected in their dreams. She also studied the effects of nutrition on sleep disturbance in menopausal women.

Always a strong dreamer, she never saw her dreams as any more than a curiosity until a personal tragedy, over twenty years ago, was foreshadowed in a dream, forcing her to take them more seriously. She has kept a daily, illustrated, dream journal ever since and has recorded in excess of 6000 dreams to date. At the end of each year she has her journal professionally bound; they make a very interesting addition to her large book collection.

In 1995, whilst still a student, she began to run regular dream workshops and has facilitated dream work groups since then, including workgroups for students studying for a Diploma in Counselling. Her first book, "Working the Nightshift, How To Understand Your Dreams", details the techniques covered in the workshops and is available from her website www.docdreamuk.com .

A member of the International Association for the Study of Dreams, (IASD), she has had articles and papers published in their magazine Dreamtime and has presented at international conferences in Europe and America. She has a particular interest in the neurobiological aspects of sleep and dreaming, having presented a paper at the IASD 21st Annual Conference in Copenhagen; "A Theoretical Perspective on the Function of REM Sleep", which explored the possibility of a link between REM sleep and the generation of new brain cells. She has also been featured in a popular women's magazine and has done a number of radio interviews. If asked whether she could have achieved so much without reference to her dreams, her answer is a resounding "no". Her dreams gave her the confidence to make major life changes, secure in the knowledge that she was making the right decision. They have been the lanterns that have illuminated the path ahead.

How to use this book

This book is designed to help you interpret your own dreams. You need to take an active role in recording and using the exercises to help you understand not only what the dreams mean but also how they can help you change your life. There are extra resources on the publisher's website, www.uolearn.com, including example sheets for recording your dreams.

Warning

This book is intended for those wishing to increase in self knowledge and become more self-aware. It is not suitable for those seeking help with problems caused by past trauma. Even where no such problems are apparent, the in depth analysis of dreams can sometimes uncover unresolved issues from the past, which may be upsetting and difficult to deal with. If any such issues arise whilst using this book, and you feel unable to deal with them alone, it is recommended that you seek professional help.

Contents

CONTENTS

Introduction

"Dreams are free, so free your dreams." Astrid Alauda

Introduction

As a child I was fascinated by my dreams and the dramas that played out in my imagination. However, it was a rather covert interest that never progressed beyond introverted entertainment. It never occurred to me that perhaps not everyone dreamed as I did and that perhaps this was the reason no one else seemed to be interested in the nocturnal goings on. Sadly I never recorded any of my dreams from that time. How fascinating and insightful it would be to read them now, all these years later. I only remember one dream from my childhood, but it was one that recurred frequently. I would find myself running down the stairs at home as fast as I could. If I ran fast enough, I would fly out of the house through the arched window above the front door and climb the clouds up to Heaven. Sometimes I reached the Angels that lived up there but sometimes I didn't. It was always very hard to climb up the clouds and there was usually something chasing me, trying to grab my feet and pull me back down. I see now that this dream was my escape from the night terrors that sometimes haunt children's dreams.

In my twenties I read John Dunne's "An Experiment with Time" in which he describes a couple of dreams that seemed to be foretelling the future. This phenomenon is now referred to as precognitive dreaming. The dreams so startled him that he conducted a series of experiments in which he invited the public to take part. I was fascinated enough to conduct my own experiments and I wasn't disappointed. I've been enthralled by this aspect of dreaming ever since. In the last ten years I have joined other interested dreamers across the globe in precognitive and telepathic dreaming experiments. If you're interested in this aspect of dreaming, you'll find links on my website.

However, my professional interest in dreams didn't start until 1993. Three years earlier I'd decided to fulfil a lifelong ambition and go to University as a full-time student. During that time, I met others who were as fascinated by dreams as I was. I spent many lunch breaks in the café bars swapping and discussing dreams. It was early on in my studies that I had a troubling dream that seemed resistant to analysis. A week later I had another one in a similar vein. It wasn't until the following week, when my brother committed suicide, that I understood what the dreams had been trying to tell me. It was then that I realised the profound importance of our dreaming life and have recorded my dreams every night since. I now have over twenty years of dream records, totalling in excess of six thousand dreams. It's fascinating to see how the dream content has changed over time, showing how my psyche has integrated, and built on, waking experiences.

After completing my degree in 1993, I embarked on doctoral research. To supplement my research funding, I asked my Local Education Authority if they would be interested in hosting a regular dream workshop. I was thrilled to get the go ahead and started running workshops the following autumn. Participants were from all walks of life with no prior experience in working with dreams. The weekly sessions involved learning and practising techniques that can be used to analyse dreams. You'll find some of these techniques in session 5 of this book. It was a rewarding experience for everyone involved and fostered deep social empathy and lasting friendships. Since then I have run similar work groups in the Midlands and also work group sessions with counselling students. It's of concern to me that many trained therapists still largely ignore the dreams of their clients. There is scientific research over the past twenty years that has proven beyond doubt that dreams are about the concerns of waking life and are a window into the mind.

There's growing evidence to support the view that dreams have a function in maintaining emotional health and that they are meaningful. There's also abundant evidence from neuroscience that the brain is unable to distinguish between real and imagined events. A dream is a real experience to the sleeping brain. Experiences change us, they mould us into who we are. Your dream experiences affect you whether you remember your dreams or not. Sadly, there are still influential academics who fail to acknowledge this growing body of evidence and continue to deny this important function of dreams. To me, the unconscious and subconscious are like the back stage workers in a theatre company, our dreams are the performances. The audience is our waking self, the "us" that operates in the everyday reality. The performances may make us laugh or cry, make us happy or sad, or leave us bewildered or unimpressed. We may even sleep through the entire performance! Whatever happens, we have the opportunity to be enriched by these performances, to learn from them and lead a more fulfilling life because of them.

There's a common misconception about dreams. It is that they are either nonsensical or simply reflections on our daily life. Yet, throughout the ages, men and women have used their dreams in order to better understand themselves, to achieve scientific breakthroughs, create great works of art, compose music and write literature. Both Freud and Jung recognised that dreams are an important route into the subconscious. If seriously explored by the dreamer, dreams can help to integrate life experiences. They can also lead to tremendous insight into human nature and human consciousness. Dreams are important. They are not just commentaries on waking events. They are meaningful and working with them can be the start of a journey to self understanding. They explore the emotion of a life situation and show us how we are experiencing that event on a psychic level. Quite often they suggest solutions to problems or ways in which we could/should modify our behaviour. They reveal our inner talents and encourage us to use them. They provide the opportunity to transform negative experiences into positive life changes. If we seriously work with even just one dream in our lifetime, we'll find something out about ourselves that will bring us closer to psychological and spiritual, health and wholeness. Dreams give us important information, providing we can understand how to use it. If you diligently work through this book and complete all the exercises, you will develop the skills you need. This course will lead you, step by step, into the depths of your psyche, draw out what's inside of you and teach you the art of understanding yourself through your dreams. You're about to embark on a journey of self discovery; it may be the most important journey you ever take.

> *"If you bring forth what is within you,*
> *what you bring forth will save you.*
>
> *If you do not bring forth what is within you,*
> *what you do not bring forth will destroy you."*

This is one of my favourite quotes (from *St Thomas's gospel*) for it states, very poetically, what psychologists have been telling us for years. That our fears, our bigotry, our disappointments, our need to love and be loved, all those things that bubble and boil in our psyche, may not kill us, but they affect our beliefs and our behaviour. These things can destroy relationships, ruin careers and bankrupt souls. Yet, when uncovered and transformed, they have the potential to move mountains, initiate acts of immense courage and bravery, and foster empathy and altruism. Let me add a cautionary note at this point. Dreams do sometimes bring unresolved past trauma into the spotlight of consciousness. If this happens to you, and you feel unable to deal with it alone, I would urge you to seek professional help from a reputable counsellor or therapist. Your family doctor will usually be able to provide you with the contact details of suitably qualified professionals.

If we take notice of our dreams, and take time to understand them, we will see that they are steering us away from those things that harm us and towards a life path that has a heart. If you've ever been to Egypt, you may have noticed how many of the statues of the Pharaohs stand with their left leg stepping forward. This was a sign, well understood within the culture at the time, that they followed the path of their heart. It was a

13

statement to the world that they lived their lives in a way that honoured themselves, the earth and all people. Of course, in the case of the Egyptian Pharaohs, this could just have been to enhance their reputation and increase their popularity! A path without a heart is hard work. It's not enjoyable. It feels wrong. It hurts you or other people, or everyone. One day you turn around and realise that you don't want to be where you are, you may even wonder how you got there. If we are to follow the path of our heart, we must "bring forth what is within us", recognise it, own it, name it, and integrate it within our being, not only for the good of ourselves but also for the people around us. You can find the signposts to this path in your dreams. If you follow them, you'll be following in the footsteps of millions of travellers who have set out before you. If you feel a little trepidation, that's good. This work is not to be taken lightly, nor must it be embarked on half-heartedly. This is serious work that will pay dividends if you succeed. To complete this Skills Training Course you'll need a sense of adventure, you'll need to be courageous, and you'll need to be willing to change, if change is what's needed.

Your first hurdle involves honesty. Often we fail to acknowledge aspects of our personality because we don't want to admit to falling short of the expectations we have of ourselves. Perhaps the most important expectation is that we should be happy with our lot in life. To say otherwise infers that we have failed in some way, or that all our past struggles were worth nothing. And so many people will tell themselves, and the world, that they are happy when actually they're not. The lies we tell ourselves are often so deeply buried in our psyche that we don't even know we're doing it. "Bringing forth what is within" will present you with such challenges. It's up to you whether you choose to uncover the truth and deal with what's there.

"Men occasionally stumble over the truth, but most of them pick themselves up and hurry off as if nothing ever happened."
Sir Winston Churchill

The second hurdle, is learning to understand the language of the subconscious; the language of dreams. I've devoted a whole session to this, in an attempt to give you a flavour of the richness and diversity of this language. Though like any foreign language we attempt to learn, this will be an ongoing endeavour. Your subconscious will always present you with new images, symbols and metaphors that need a little work to decipher. Some dreams are easy to understand, others are more difficult, even to those experienced in working with dreams. Prepare to be challenged.

When you've completed this course, I suggest you work your way through the further recommended reading in order to expand your knowledge and gain further insight. Dreams are multi-faceted and multi-dimensional and it's impossible to do justice to all their aspects in a book such as this. If you feel the need to engage with others in sharing your dreams, and I strongly recommend that you do, you'll find many dream networking sites on the internet, or you could simply share your dreams with like-minded friends. Whatever you choose to do, I hope you enjoy working through this book as much as I enjoyed writing it.

Unconscious versus subconscious

Throughout the book I have used both of these words in such a way that the reader may have the impression they are used interchangeably. They are not. There has been ongoing debate for many years about the difference between these two terms, but no consensus of opinion has emerged and the debate continues. It could be argued that such categorisations are completely arbitrary anyway and are attempting to describe things that actually are not separate entities. Consciousness is better likened to a continuum, with fully awake at one end and no signs of life at the other. However, if we are to discuss the workings of the psyche we must use some intellectual terms to try and put what we are saying into a comprehensible framework. Such is the case in this book and so, to avoid confusion, I have chosen to define the terms in the following way. Others may use different definitions. I do not claim to be the final authority on this matter.

Unconscious – the part of the mind of which we are totally unaware. For instance, we may exhibit unconscious tendencies. An example may be someone with a phobia but with no idea why. Another example may be the behavioural information carried within our genetic makeup; compare Jung's Collective Unconscious.

Subconscious – the part of the mind lying just below consciousness. With a little help these things can be brought into consciousness. An example would be intuition or gut feelings.

Throughout the book I assume that dreams arise from the subconscious, purely to avoid unnecessary repetition of both terms. Bear in mind that unconscious elements can also be incorporated into dreams.

Session 1:
Dreams are more
than you think

"Dreams say what they mean, but they don't
say it in daytime language." Gail Godwin

Session 1: Dreams are more than you think

1.1: Dream dictionaries

Before we begin to work on our dreams; a word about the ubiquitous dream dictionaries. It's possible to attempt a superficial interpretation of some dreams with very little knowledge of dream language. Modern dream dictionaries are popular because they give dreamers a quick answer. However, their content is dependent on the knowledge and traditions of the culture in which they originated. For example, modern Western society is not like Ancient Egyptian society, nor has it the values of the Victorians. Some have their origins in Gypsy folklore and tend to assume that dreams are divinatory; that is, that they always tell the future. None of them can ever elucidate personal symbolism so you need to bear this in mind if you're ever tempted to use them.

Successful dream analysis, or interpretation, rests entirely on uncovering the intimate relationship between the dreamer and the dream. This can only be achieved by the dreamer exploring the dream within the context of their own life and experiences. In view of this, I do not generally endorse the use of dream dictionaries. However, as you begin to explore your dreams, you may sometimes find yourself unable to make any personal connection to a particular dream image. In such cases, a modern edition that offers sensible, psychologically-based, suggestions and comments can sometimes provide thoughtful prompts which can then facilitate personal associations. The one I would recommend is Dream Dictionary: An A to Z Guide to understanding your unconscious mind by Tony Crisp

1.2: Warming up exercises

Before we begin the challenging business of dream analysis, let's begin with a couple of warming up exercises to get you in the mood for the work that lies ahead.

Exercise 1: Dreams about Food

Read the two dreams that follow and jot down what you think the dreams might mean.

Don't be tempted to look at the suggested interpretations until you've completed this exercise.

Dream 1

I was looking at a vine growing up a sort of trellis. I noticed there were three branches at the top and, as I looked, the buds on them burst open and a flower came out, and then bunches of ripe grapes. They looked really delicious. I had a cup in my hand and I started to press the grapes into the cup to get the juice out. I then noticed that my employer was standing by me and I gave the cup to him.

Your interpretation:

....

....

....

....

....

....

....

Dream 2

I was walking along a quiet country lane balancing three white baskets on my head, stacked one on top of the other. I knew that the baskets contained lots of different types of bread and I was taking them to my boss's house. As I walked along, I became aware that birds were swooping down and eating all the bread out of the baskets.

Your interpretation:

....

....

....

....

....

....

....

Suggested interpretations:

Dream 1

The image of a healthy vine growing up a trellis might suggest organisation, success and prosperity. Healthy vines mean lots of wine, leading to high profit and social enjoyment. This suggests something is blossoming and bearing fruit. As the dreamer takes the juice from the grapes and gives it to his/her employer, this might suggest a very productive relationship.

Dream 2

The baskets of bread, carried on top of the head, seem to be a good symbol until we hear that the birds swoop down and eat all the contents. There's nothing left to give to their employer. As bread is a basic, staple food, having none left may suggest impoverishment and a lack of sustenance. If we think in terms of the birds stealing the bread, this may suggest the dreamer is feeling cheated or is about to have something of immense importance stolen from him/her.

In summary, dream 1 appears to be positive and indicative of success in an undertaking. However, dream 2 does not sound so good and suggests that things may not work out too well.

How did you do?

If you haven't guessed, both those dreams are very old, from biblical times.

They dreamed a dream both of them, each man his dream in one night, each man according to the interpretation of his dream, the butler and the baker of the king of Egypt, which were bound in the prison. And Joseph came in unto them in the morning, and looked upon them, and, behold, they were sad. And he asked Pharaoh's officers that were with him in the ward of his lord's house, saying, "Wherefore look ye so sadly today?" And they said unto him, "We have dreamed a dream, and there is no interpreter of it." And Joseph said unto them, "Do not interpretations belong to God? Tell me them, I pray you." The chief butler told his dream to Joseph, and said to him, "In my dream, behold, a vine was before me."

In the vine were three branches: and it was as though it budded, and her blossoms shot forth; and the clusters thereof brought forth ripe grapes:

The Pharaoh's cup was in my hand: and I took the grapes, and pressed them into Pharaoh's cup, and I gave the cup into Pharaoh's hand.

Joseph said him, "This is the interpretation of it: The three branches are three days: Yet within three days shall Pharaoh lift up thine head, and restore thee unto thy place: and thou shalt deliver Pharaoh's cup into his hand, after the former manner when you were his butler. But think on me when it shall be well with thee, and show kindness, I pray thee, unto me, and make mention of me unto Pharaoh, and bring me out of this house: For indeed I was stolen away out of the land of the Hebrews: and here also have I done nothing that they should put me into the dungeon.

When the chief baker saw that the interpretation was good, he said to Joseph, "I also was in my dream, and, behold, I had three white baskets on my head. In the uppermost basket there was of all manner of bakemeats for Pharaoh; and the birds ate them out of the basket upon my head. And Joseph answered and said, "This is the interpretation: The three baskets are three days. Yet within three days shall Pharaoh lift up thy head from off thee, and shall hang thee on a tree; and the birds shall eat thy flesh from off thee." It came to pass the third day, which was Pharaoh's birthday, that he made a feast unto all his servants: and he lifted up the head of the chief butler and of the chief baker among his servants.

He restored the chief butler unto his butlership again; and he gave the cup into Pharaoh's hand. But he hanged the chief baker: as Joseph had interpreted to them.

This account of Joseph's interpretation of the Baker's and the Butler's dreams clearly reflects the cultural meanings of several images described in the Chester Beatty Papyrus, an Egyptian book of dream interpretation which dates back to 2000 BC In fact, birds, which Joseph interpreted as foreboding ill for the steward, are still commonly interpreted as symbols of death in much of South America and this is still a common interpretation found in some dream dictionaries.

In the ancient world, members of the community, who showed a special knowledge of the dream world, like Daniel and Joseph, were assigned as dream interpreters. Dream libraries existed in Nineveh as long ago as 5000 BC and the Chester Beatty papyrus shows that dream interpretation was also well established in Egypt. Hieroglyphic inscriptions that recorded fragments of dreams and dream-meanings were common place.

Interest in dreams was maintained throughout the centuries but the production of printed books in the 15th Century revolutionised the practice of working with dreams. Suddenly, those with no experience of dream interpretation could access, what we now call, dream dictionaries, and interpret their own dreams. These books were mainly based on Artemidorus of Daldis, a famous 2nd Century Greek writer, and they contained his cultural interpretations of many dream symbols.

With the rise of Freudian and Jungian psychology in the early 20th Century, it was recognised that dreams contain complex ideas that are very personal to the life of the dreamer. Although many different schools of psychoanalytical theory developed around these ideas, they all had one thing in common; that dreams needed to be interpreted or analysed with reference to the life experiences of the dreamer.

Today, many of the psychoanalytical theories about dreams, including Freud's theory that all dreams are wish fulfilments, have fallen out of favour. What we are left with, is a certainty that dreams are very personal to the dreamer and that they address issues relevant to the dreamer's life. No one but the dreamer can know the unique meaning of the images that rise up from their subconscious. A black dog in my dream is likely to mean something completely different to a black dog in your dream. You may have had this black dog as a pet and so have pleasant associations. You may be tempted to tell me that the dog in my dream represents devotion and loyalty. However, a black dog may have bitten me when I was a child. So who's the best person to interpret the meaning of the black dog in my dream?

This brings me to my golden rule of dream interpretation.

> **Other people can help you to explore your dreams and may even be able to give you a useful overview.**
> **However, the only person who can really know what a dream means is the dreamer.**

Everything else is personal projection and says more about the person offering the interpretation, than the dreamer. I ask that you be aware of this should you ever be tempted to interpret someone else's dream for them.

Exercise 2: Your first dream analysis

I now want you to write down a dream that you remember having in the past. Write it down in as much detail as you can remember. If that's very little, don't worry, whatever you remember will be useful. After doing this, jot down an overview of your feelings about the dream and what you think it might have been about. If you haven't got a clue, just write down that you don't know. You'll be returning to this dream later in the course, at which time you'll be able to look at it with new understanding.

Description of a dream you've had:

....

....

....

....

....

....

....

....

What do you think the dream was telling you?

....

....

....

....

....

....

....

....

....

1.3: Eliminating superficial beliefs about dreams

There is a tendency to dismiss the components of a dream as being unimportant and unworthy of individual consideration. This attitude can distort and even sabotage attempts to understand what we see. Think of a dream as a gift that's contained within many layers of packaging. If you want to see the gift, you must first remove the wrapping paper, layer by layer, and then hold it up to the light for closer examination. Listening to dreams discussed in casual conversation, it's clear that many people are happy to give a superficial interpretation of their dreams based on what Freud called day residue. This is like looking at the wrapping paper and thinking it is the present.

Let me give an example. A lady mentioned one day that she'd dreamed the previous night of walking round an abattoir and that she'd woken from the dream feeling very frightened. She described in graphic detail what she'd seen there and went on to explain that, on the evening of the dream, she'd watched a documentary about Sweeney Todd. In her opinion, this was why she'd had the dream and so concluded it had no meaning in terms of her own life. She refuted all suggestions that this dream might be important. Such superficial interpretations, and a resistance to examine the dream in more detail, can indicate that there is an underlying issue that the dreamer is not facing up to, and may not even be aware of. Certainly this is true for any dream with a nightmarish quality. In this case, you can be certain that the issue will be causing difficulties in the dreamer's life. The effects can not only be seen in the general well-being of the person, but also in their behaviour, attitudes and beliefs about themselves and life in general. In the case of the abattoir, it would have been very helpful for the lady if she'd been prepared to ask herself questions like, "In what area of my life do I feel I'm being cut to pieces / sacrificed / treated like a piece of meat?" or even, "Why? If this dream was about Sweeney Todd, why didn't I dream of human carcasses, murder, or meat pies?"

Four principles of dream interpretation:

✓ **Always** assume that your dream has meaning beyond its face value and commit to uncovering that meaning.

✓ **Never** judge the dream when recording it. If you do, you will likely add things in or take things out. If you're tempted to dismiss a part of a dream, make a special effort to record it in detail. It's the things our conscious ego, (the part of you that you think of as "I"), thinks are not important that often hold the key to something the ego doesn't want to face up to. The ego is a very powerful censor and will try and dismiss everything and anything that doesn't support its self image, (more of this later).

✓ **Honour** your dreams by giving them the attention they deserve. They will reward you a hundred fold.

✓ **Take ownership** of your dream. It's your property, your responsibility. Only **you** can really know what it means.

Session 2:
Understanding the language of dreams

"Dreams are illustrations... from the book your soul is writing about you." Marsha Norman

Session 2: Understanding the language of dreams

2.1: The language of dreams

In the last session I talked briefly about the use of dream dictionaries to interpret dreams. I explained that most of these dictionaries are based on cultural or historical associations, many having their roots in gypsy folklore or superstition. Although they can be very entertaining, they can only offer superficial, and often misleading, interpretations. It's true that, as human beings, we all experience life events in very similar ways and so our dreams do display commonalities that have a similar meaning for everyone who dreams them.

However, your dream contains symbols and images from your subconscious; it's your story. It's crucial that you understand all the implications of this statement before we go any further. You are the script writer, the director, the producer, and casting director of your dreams and the stuff you put in them is there because it has a personal, and often unique, meaning for you. You are also the actors, the props, the stage scenery and the audience.

The authors of dream dictionaries, and those wanting to tell you what your dreams mean, have no knowledge of the "you" that has scripted your dream. They don't live inside your head, and they don't know what life experiences you've had. Your dreams are the product of your own personal symbolism and, because of this, I want to reiterate the Golden Rule of dream analysis. Only the dreamer can fully and correctly interpret the dream. Your dreams are very personal messages from yourself to yourself and, as such, you are the only person qualified to fully, and accurately, interpret your dreams.

Before you can interpret your dreams, you must learn their language. Dreams are often hard to understand because they don't use familiar, everyday language. Reading a dream report can be rather like trying to translate a letter from a foreign penpal who has grown up in a culture that you have little knowledge of and who doesn't speak your native language very well. Dreams are the language of the unconscious. It's a language of symbols, puns, parables and metaphors. They are the product of a part of you that is more ingenious, more creative and more beautiful than you give yourself credit for. Once grasped, the language is simplicity itself, and yet an understanding of that simplicity can be so very elusive.

The part of your mind that dreams does not see your everyday reality as the "wakeful you" sees it. It experiences only the emotions that are stirred as you go about your daily life. From these emotions, it forms concepts and produces a cornucopia of literal stories to try and make sense of it all. To understand these stories you must first understand yourself and, to help you in this task, session 3 will guide you through a process, whereby you'll be able to find out a little more about the "you" of your everyday world.

Dreams Are Complex

Dreams operate on many different levels and one dream can often address more than one life issue at the same time, blending everything that is presently of interest. Sometimes, you'll be satisfied to take the dream story at face value; described by Freud as the manifest content. Yet there will be dreams where you instinctively know there is more to understand and so you will want to investigate the latent (or hidden) content by exploring the symbols and emotions in more depth. Doing this can reveal how inconsequential aspects of a dream can sometimes carry within them profound, emotional associations that can lead to a deep understanding of self and a treasure house of wisdom.

The good news is that successful dream analysis doesn't need any intellectual or academic input and, in fact, is probably benefited when these are absent.

So, let us look more closely at the language of dreams.

2.2: Symbols

Dreams are a collection of images and symbols assembled into a story. Often the meaning of the story evades us but by looking at the symbols and asking ourselves what they mean to us personally, we can start to unravel the meaning. It's like looking at the individual images woven into a tapestry to get a better understanding about the meaning of the entire work. Everything that is in your dream is significant and very relevant to the dream story. Nothing is chosen at random.

What is a symbol?

Symbols represent more than their physical appearance. They are a very economical language that can describe and express a vast and subtle range of human feelings and motivations in one object. They can lead us to explore an idea or situation that's currently too ill-defined to be grasped by the conscious mind. Although, there are universal symbols that many people recognise and experience in similar ways (religious icons are a good example) most dream symbols are very personal to the dreamer. So only the dreamer can decide why their subconscious might have chosen that particular image, above any other.

Take, for example, the image of a clown. One of my nephews developed a phobia about clowns because of a silly incident that happened when he was watching a Christmas circus at age five. The clown, looking fearsome to such a small child, came towards him with a jaunty walk, nodding his head, pointing at him, asking him to stand up and join him in the circus ring. My nephew was terrified, jumped up from his seat and hid under it. No amount of persuasion would get him out and eventually the family had to leave. Clearly, the appearance of a clown in his adult dreams would be tapping into the anxiety that he experienced all those years ago. In this case, it would be safe to assume that the dream clown is symbolising something in the present that is demanding his participation, but of which he is fearful and anxious.

This is not to say that whatever is represented by the clown is bad or menacing in itself, it's just eliciting the same emotions in him. It may be a great opportunity or it may be something to be avoided. Exploration of the dream will uncover which it is. If he remains unaware of the reason for his anxiety, he may well make the wrong decision. For someone else, the image of a clown may bring back wonderful memories of a protected and carefree childhood and remind the dreamer of a particularly happy time in their life.

Whatever the symbol, it's very important to take note of the details contained within the image. So, for instance, what was the clown wearing? Where were they? What were they doing? Did they look happy/sad/menacing? If it reminds you of a real experience, how does the dream differ from that experience? It's not enough to simply make associations to the words, as dream dictionaries do; the associations must begin from the point of the unique dream image. If we dream of a rose, for example, our dream rose will not be any old rose; it will be a statement within itself and will possess qualities not necessarily seen in all roses. So, it may be red, or pink, or white. It may have a scent. It may be a single rose or one of a whole bunch. It may be fresh or it may be old and wilting, growing in a garden or displayed in a vase. Whatever its state, it will remind you of something or will elicit a specific emotion within you.

Think of a dream symbol as an effective expression of something that the subconscious fully understands, but the conscious mind has yet to recognise. If you struggle to appreciate the significance of any particular symbol in your dream, ask yourself, "Why?" Why that particular symbol and not another? For instance if you sit on a three-legged stool in your dream, why was the stool not a chair? What is it about the stool that's different to a chair? When would you sit on a stool instead of a chair? Remember, dream analysis is all about discovering what lies in the subconscious and so you need to look beyond the facade.

2.3: Metaphors

Metaphorical associations, rather than spoken language, are the language of the unconscious; used to express and elucidate our experiences. It's the language of poets and artists and transcends culture and race barriers. This universal language is capable of being understood by everyone on a subconscious level, whether we consciously recognise it or not.

A metaphor is when something is described as though it were something else. For instance, I might say, "She's a barrel of laughs," to describe a woman with a happy outlook who is always making jokes. Clearly, I'm not suggesting that she looks like a barrel that makes a laughing sound, but this is how she may be portrayed in my dreams! This is a simple example, of a common metaphor, but abstract concepts can be described or explained in the same way. For instance, "the heart of the matter" isn't really a pulsating organ at the centre of a problem. "Grass root politics" doesn't mean we're concerned about the state of our lawns and "getting to the root of a problem" doesn't mean you have to start digging up trees or vegetables.

Metaphors are used all the time in our everyday life and they really are the stuff of our dreams. Listen out for metaphorical statements the next time you have a conversation. You'll be surprised at how often we all use them. In fact, our everyday language consists almost entirely of metaphors. We seem to link our experiences quite naturally to associated images. So, for instance, we often refer to arguments in terms of war "I never win an argument", "Let battle commence" or even in terms of a journey, "I have set out to prove," "We have arrived at an agreement." All of these are metaphorical statements.

Common Metaphors

Many of these metaphorical associations are in common usage. People sharing a common culture will, at one time or another, have used them and fully understand what they mean when they hear other people use them. Take, for example, the feeling of not being able to cope; the person may say that they feel they are "falling apart" or "going to pieces." Their friends might say "pull yourself together" or "get a grip of yourself." Taken literally, these statements are nonsensical and yet they communicate, very well, emotions that are too nebulous to be described in any other way. So, it's very easy for us to express the concerns of everyday life in this way and we all do it, all of the time.

Dream Metaphors

Most dreams are a long series of individual, personal metaphors that can be difficult to disentangle, because they are not confined to those metaphors that are in common usage. In addition, each individual metaphorical image may have more than one interpretation on a conscious level and the interpretation will, therefore, be dependent upon other things within the dream and the dream story.

Dream metaphors are better described as conceptual metaphors, born from personal memories, expectations and experiences of the person who dreamt them. To the conscious mind, they may seem arbitrary and incoherent and, therefore, difficult to understand. This is because they arise spontaneously in the subconscious, from abstract thoughts, and comprise of sensory-derived images that are not directed by waking consciousness. For example, suppose a dream deals with the anxiety felt about embarking on a new venture. One of the metaphors that may be used in the dream is "sailing into uncharted waters", in which case, the dream imagery may be of a sea voyage in an alien landscape. The dreamer may find himself or herself in a large ship or a small punt. They may be on the open sea, an inland lake or a turbulent river. The water may be clear or muddy, calm or choppy. The sailing vessel may be in good repair or falling apart and taking in water. There may be obstacles to overcome or it may all be plain sailing. In other words, the subconscious feelings about this new venture will be woven into a story around the central theme of a voyage over water.

Emotional Climate Metaphors

In addition, the environment, or the weather, in the dream may also be metaphorical. So, for instance, a stormy sky may be an emotional climate metaphor, in which interior emotions are portrayed by exterior weather conditions. How often do we say of a difficult situation, "the storm clouds are gathering" or "I'm weathering the storm." Similarly, when we're in a situation that we feel is beyond our control, we may dream of a hurricane or a tidal wave that threatens to destroy us. If we're apprehensive about something, we may dream of "the calm before the storm" to convey the feeling of impending emotional discord. Dreaming of "clouds with silver linings" expresses our feeling that good things can come out of a bad situation. These emotional climate metaphors are used all the time and so it's very important, when recording your dream, to take note of the climate, environment and weather conditions that prevail during the dream. Your subconscious is in receipt of all available information about a certain situation; so the climate metaphor used in the dream may be different to the one you would choose consciously. Exploring such discrepancies can be the key to unravelling a difficult life issue.

2.4: Puns

A pun is a play on words and dreams are very good at producing some excellent ones. Sometimes they take the form of using the same word but in a different sense. An example would be a friend, who you totally rely on (your rock), taking you to a rock concert in your dream. Sometimes puns use a different word for the same sense. For instance, someone who has cheated on you may appear in your dream as a cheetah.

Taking the examples given here, you can see that if these occurred within a dream, their subtle meanings or inference could be easily overlooked. One of the most amusing examples from my own dreams occurred at a time when I was going through a marriage break up and trying to juggle life as a single parent with work commitments. When things went wrong, or I felt I wasn't managing as well as I should have been, I would say to my friends, "My life's going to pot!" or "I'm going to pot!" This is a common Lancashire saying that means one is no longer in control of events and things are becoming chaotic. In the dream I was driving my car (me going through my life), which needed petrol (energy) when I passed a signpost that said, "Welcome to Pot." This dream certainly lifted my spirits, reminding me that underneath all the stress and worry, I still had my sense of humour! It's also worth mentioning that there were other things in this dream that suggested ways in which I could manage my life better.

2.5: Parables

A parable is a simple story that tells a moral or spiritual truth. They can be found in many religious texts and moral stories such as Aesop's fables. They are usually thought provoking because they challenge preconceptions and often result in a change of belief or attitude. Parables use analogy to simplify complex ideas and, like puns, are a natural vehicle for the subconscious to express itself. Unfortunately, recognising when a dream is in the form of a parable can be difficult, and sometimes does not become apparent until weeks or even years later. If you think you have a dream that may contain an important lesson, try re-writing it in the form of a parable. If there's a lesson there, this should make it clear.

For example, take the following dream:

I'm at the meat counter in my local supermarket. There's so much choice. I ask the assistant what all the different cuts of meat are, what they weigh and how much they cost. He's annoyed by all my questions; tells me he's too busy to spend time helping me to make up my mind. He tells me to pick just one thing and then he'll give me all the details about it.

Re-written as a parable:

A woman goes into a supermarket looking for good quality meat that will also give her value for money. There's a lot of choice but she's no idea what the different cuts are, nor what they might cost. She asks a lot of questions, trying to ascertain which cut will give her the best deal. The Assistant tells her that first she must decide what she wants, only then will he tell her what it will cost.

2.6: Themes

All dreams have a theme running through them. Some themes are very easy to recognise; the so-called Universal or archetypal dream themes (see below). These are thought to have their basis in common human experiences based on biological, genetic and cultural heritage as well as personal experience and local subcultures.

For example, if we dream about being attacked by a vampire, it's unlikely it would have any other meaning than the obvious one, which is that someone or something is taking something from us without our permission; perhaps energy or money or power. So, the theme may be described as feeling drained or perhaps being sucked dry.

Others may be more elusive. For instance, water will nearly always represent the state of the dreamer's emotions, so a dream about your house flooding may suggest that emotions, normally under control, are adversely affecting your private life or feelings of security. Being hit by a tidal wave will usually mean that the dreamer is in fear of being overwhelmed by powerful emotions that are already out of control. Here the theme may be described as, overwhelmed or out of control. Identifying the theme can give you a simple image to focus on and this alone will usually give you a good idea as to what the dream is about. Examining other aspects of the dream in more detail will reveal additional information that should clarify the situation further.

When you become familiar with your own personal symbolism, this process will become much easier. You'll also start to notice that some themes recur in your dreams. These are always worthy of special attention.

Universal Dream Themes

There are dream themes that are common to all of humanity, regardless of culture or ancestry. For instance, dreams of being chased or attacked are a common response to the stresses of life everywhere and are closely associated with the physiological fight or flight response. The personal situation from which the dream arises may differ from person to person but the emotional response of the psyche seems always to be the same. As Patricia Garfield so colourfully states:

"Like a hearty stew that is rich with local produce, the universal dreams differ among different peoples, but they are all nourishing variants of the same wholesome meal. They are as old as humanity and as widespread as our globe."

In many ways, it's comforting to know that you were not alone last night when you dreamed you were being chased through the shadowlands; millions of people on Earth were probably having a very similar dream. It's our fears that pursue us through the dreamtime, fears that we are not facing up to. Your fears may be different to mine and your pursuer may look different and chase you through different landscapes, despite these differences, the underlying experience is the same. Or perhaps we dream that someone has died and wake up concerned that a real death is imminent. Again, this is a universal dream experience that indicates that something, usually a relationship, is coming to an end. For some reason, human beings seem to be predisposed to interpret certain life situations using very similar metaphors. So, the monsters that chase us in our dreams are the monsters of the mind, or the shadows of Jungian psychology. They are born of fear, anxiety, anger and hatred and are given symbolic form. The psychological and biological response to these emotions is to fight or run away depending on how confident we are of winning the battle. In our dreams most of us, as in waking life, seem to run away. Just as common a dream theme is pregnancy. These dreams usually stem from feelings that we are about to "give birth" to a new idea or a new way of life. At least twelve universal dream themes are now recognised, but it is only by examining the dream in detail that we can pinpoint the specific area of life to which the dream relates. For a list see www.patriciagarfield.com/publications/udreams_99dreamtime16.htm

Universal dream themes apart, the majority of dreams have a theme that is unique to the dreamer and so have to be interpreted individually.

2.7: Colour

Colour is as important in dreams as it is in our daily lives. Our mood can be affected by it, whether or not we are aware of it. Not only that, but we can change our perception of the colours that we see around us. Anyone who has suffered from depression will know how grey and colourless the world appears when we're feeling pessimistic about the future. On the other hand, when we're really happy colours can appear vibrant and alive.

The language of colour is usually consistent, within a cultural setting, and we use colour symbolism all the time to explain how we are feeling. Think of familiar expressions such as *feeling blue*, used to convey a feeling of sadness. When we're angry and about to lose control we talk about *seeing red*. If we describe someone or something as *red hot* we give the impression that it excites our passion; what about *green with envy* when we're jealous or in a *black mood* when we're feeling irritable and depressed? We might say that someone sees life in terms of *black and white*, meaning they are rather rigid in their thinking, or perhaps that they have great clarity of thought. Have you ever really thought about the meaning behind these words? Such phrases weren't just picked out of the air; they actually reflect the fact that colours have emotional connotations.

Certain colours can alleviate stress, tension, anxiety and depression whilst others can bring on those emotional states. For instance, red décor is sometimes used in the meeting rooms of more progressive businesses, as this colour is known to excite the imagination and raise energy levels. So, it's not a colour you should be using in your bedroom; unless of course you don't intend to do very much sleeping in there! The pale pastel shades tend to be calming, particularly green, blue and lilac. These colours are often used in clinical settings; such as hospitals.

Exercise 3: Working with colour

This exercise will help you to discover your own personal associations to different colours. When a particular colour appears in your dream, you'll be able to identify the emotion driving the dream without too much difficulty. Read through the list of emotions in the Table below and assign a colour to each one. There are no right or wrong answers to this. Our associations with colour are not just instinctive; there are also psychological factors that affect how colours make us feel. These factors may be very personal and will often be influenced by subconscious impressions formed in emotionally charged situations - situations that may have been happy or sad. Don't give too much thought to your answers; your first, gut response is usually the most reliable. If you're having trouble doing this by just reading the words, try doing it the other way round, using coloured paper or card. Meditate on each colour in turn. How does it make you feel? What associations do you have? How would you feel if your lounge was decorated entirely in that colour?

Emotion	Associated colour
Anger	
Despair	
Joy	
Peace	
Love	
Hate	
Calm	
Energetic	
Sadness	
Fear	
Passion	
Enthusiasm	

Session 3:
Practical Skills

"Dreams are nature's answering service - don't forget to pick up your messages once in a while." Sarah Crestinn

Session 3: Practical Skills

3.1: Remembering your dreams

To work on your dreams, you need to remember them. Some people find remembering difficult, or find that they go for long periods when they don't remember any dreams at all. Researchers have identified many factors that influence whether or not we find it easy to remember our dreams. The most important of these are sleep quality, life-style, stress, creativity and your attitude towards dreams. If you're having trouble remembering your dreams, you'll find hints and tips in this section that will help to improve your dream recall. If you're really determined to remember at least one dream every night then you probably will. It's also very helpful to train yourself so that the first thing you think of when you wake up is "What was I dreaming?" Make sure you have something to hand on which to record them!

Your attitude to dreams

This is the easiest factor to control. If you don't believe your dreams are important, you'll rarely remember them, so take them seriously; honour them. You'll find that the more you work with your dreams, even if it's only working with fragments of half-remembered dreams, the easier they will be to remember in the future. You can also try a little NLP (Neuro Linguistic Programming). This involves consciously programming your brain with new neural pathways. In this case, you need to instill into your mind that you will remember your dreams on waking. Simple commands such as, "I **will** remember my dreams," or a statement of fact such as, "I **do** remember my dreams," or "I always remember my dreams" are particularly effective. You need to repeat the affirmation many times during the day and, with persistence, there's no reason why you will not remember four or five dreams every night. You could also try viewing your subconscious as the best friend you ever had, a friend whose main purpose in life is to help you. You don't have to take your friend's advice but you would want to do them the courtesy of listening to what they have to say, even though sometimes they might reveal some home truths about you that you'd prefer not to know! Respect your dreams.

Sleep Quality

Your sleeping brain will conjure up far more than four or five dreams a night, but you're only likely to remember the dreams that occur during the last REM (Rapid Eye Movement) period before waking. REM periods occur approximately every ninety minutes and get longer as the night wears on, with the early hours of the morning being the time when most dreaming occurs. Hence, the quality of sleep affects dream recall. Nocturnal awakenings are common during light sleep which is why many people say they remember their dreams if they are sleeping away from home or in an anxious state of mind. If you're really determined to remember as many dreams as possible you can set an alarm clock to wake you at the end of every REM period; the first one occurs about 90 minutes after falling asleep. There are devices on the market that are designed to wake you gently, usually by flashing lights inside an eyepiece, every time they detect a period of REM, (signalled by moving eyelids). This is a bit extreme for most people and the devices are still rather expensive and certainly not necessary.

Creativity

Many activities such as talking, reading and maths stimulate analytical thoughts (often labelled left brain activity). The more creative side of your thinking is stimulated by activities such as relaxation, drawing, looking at pictures and physical activities that are repetitive (labelled as right brain activities). Any activity before sleep that stimulates your creativity will tend to enhance your dreaming life.

Listening to music, pursuing creative arts, practising meditation or using relaxation techniques before bed are all useful in enhancing recall. Most people report that dream recall can be increased simply by reading a book about dreams at bedtime. If you don't consider yourself to be a particularly creative person, it's likely that your left brain dominates your thought processes and you may find it difficult to remember your dreams. This doesn't disbar you from remembering, it just means that you might have to work a bit harder at practising right-brain activation techniques before going to bed.

Lifestyle

I'm sure everyone reading this book is aware of the importance of a good, work/life balance. Draw a pie chart of the different aspects of your life. If it's all work, and/or commitments to family and friends, it might be a good idea to timetable in some "me" time.

Lives that are very busy, leave no time for reflection, and no time for remembering dreams. We all need time for reflection if we want to have some control over where we're going with our lives; space to think about what we're doing, why we're doing it, and what we want in our future. This relaxation time can be used to work with your dreams, and doing this will help you remember them more often. I taught in an FE college for many years and can sympathise with the demands of a hectic, daily routine. Staying up late and getting up very early in order to get through one's workload, is not conducive to remembering dreams. If this is your life, then just commit to working with your dreams during vacations, when the daily grind subsides a little.

Stress

If you're suffering from stress or anxiety, it's likely you'll be having lots of dreams; some of which may wake you in the early hours of the morning. Recording your dreams during this difficult time can be a very healthy and healing thing to do and I would encourage you in this wholeheartedly. The emotions of stress and anxiety, and also depression, are wake-up calls. There's something wrong in some area of your life and it's making you ill. Working with your dreams will not only help you identify the real cause of the problem, (not always the same as our conscious view), but will also suggest ways in which you can deal with the problem to improve your life. If you're taking antidepressant medication, you will probably be aware that many of the antidepressants can significantly reduce the amount of time spent in REM sleep. However, you should still be able to remember enough dreams to help you in your recovery.

When you wake, don't move

If you are having trouble remembering your dreams, a really useful tip is not to change your position whilst you're trying to recall them. A dream that is only vaguely remembered will slip away before you've turned your head on the pillow. If you do move, as doubtless you will until you get used to it, you must return immediately to the position you were in when you woke. By doing this, you will often be able to re-capture it. Once remembered, a dream must be recorded immediately. It's very tempting to go over the dream in your mind, especially if you wake in the middle of the night, and believe that you will remember it later. The chances are that you won't, unless it was a very vivid, or frightening, dream but even then a lot of the detail will be lost. There's nothing more frustrating than the vague memory of a dream now forgotten. If this happens, it's important that you record whatever you remember, even if it's only a vague recollection of a feeling or a colour. By doing this you will be sending yourself a very powerful message that you are serious about honouring your dreams.

3.2: Recording your dreams

Remembering dreams isn't enough – you'll also need to record them if you want to explore their meaning later. It's important that you keep recording materials or equipment close to hand when you go to bed. If using pen and paper, often the best place is under your pillow, enabling you to scribble out a remembered dream without too much movement and without opening your eyes too wide. You'll find that as soon as you open your eyes and begin to register that you are fully conscious, the dream will slip quickly and silently away. If using a voice recorder, make sure you choose one that has a record button that's easy to identify by touch alone. I wouldn't recommend that you use the "voice activated" command. If you do, you'll likely record an awful lot of unwanted nocturnal noises!

What to record

What you record is probably more important than how you record it. My advice is to record everything you can remember. As auditory information is often the first thing to be forgotten, it's a good idea to record what you hear in the dream before anything else. Similarly, anything that you see written in a dream should be recorded as quickly as possible. Auditory and textual information takes many forms; it may be a street name, a person's name, a piece of poetry, a question or a conversation. If you delay recording these until you reach the part of the dream where they occurred, you'll often find you've forgotten it completely. Don't worry too much, at this stage, about the order of events in the dream; you can tidy it up later. Try and recount as much of the detail as possible; including details of the environment, the weather, the décor of a room, the clothes worn by the dream characters and any colours that particularly stand out. It's also a good idea to record what feelings and emotions were revealed in the dream and also how you felt when you awoke from it. For example; if you woke up feeling angry, lonely, happy; the feeling will undoubtedly be connected to the last dream you had. This detail can be added later in the day if you find yourself short of time in the mornings. Of course, you could always set your alarm for five minutes earlier! Make sure you date the dream record and, if possible, make a note of the time you had the dream. This is important if you record a dream in the middle of the night because research has indicated that dreams dreamed on the same night tend to deal with the same issue, with each dream in the sequence following on from the previous dream.

How to record

Before you embark on the work described later in this book, you need to decide how you're going to record your dreams. You'll need to set up the system beforehand, so it's ready for your first dream.

There are many different ways to do this; none of them are right or wrong. Some may work better than others, but the final decision is yours; use whatever method suits you best.

The first draft

Make a record of your dream whilst you're still at the "coal face" so to speak. If you don't do this, you'll either forget the dream entirely or will only remember a few snatches; both of these outcomes can cause a great deal of frustration, not to mention the potential loss of valuable insights. Make the record in whatever form you find easiest. There are many ways you might choose to do this; choose one that suits your circumstances.

If you find yourself short of time in the mornings, you could simply jot down the key words, though be warned, these are sometimes insufficient to stimulate full recall of the dream. You could write out a full transcript, though obviously this requires much more time. Making quick sketches of important scenes or images is essential, so make sure you always do this, even if this is the only record you make. I choose to use a digital recorder, which allows me to record immense detail; virtually nothing is lost. It's also much quicker to speak your dream rather than write it out. If you're going to use pen and paper, I recommend that you purchase a pen with an in-built light, especially if you don't sleep alone. It will allow you to record your dreams in the darkness without disturbing either yourself or your partner too much. Keep the pen and paper close to hand; under your pillow is probably the best place. If you put them on a bedside table, make sure there's nothing on there that can be knocked over as you fumble about in the darkness.

I've lost many a dream through the shock of knocking a glass of water over in the middle of the night as I search for my Dictaphone! In the morning, if you've time, jot down a few notes on what is currently happening in your life; the issues you are concerning yourself with and anything that is worrying you. I also recommend that you record whatever was on your mind when you drifted off to sleep; not always the easiest thing to remember!

Whichever method you choose, don't worry about the neatness or otherwise of the record, you can always re-write it, re-draw it, type it into your computer or otherwise neaten it up later.

Final record

Make time, at regular intervals, to transform your rough notes/ voice recordings into an organised record that makes the dreams accessible and easy to work with. It helps to rewrite the dream in the present tense as this has the effect of placing you back into the dream and makes the story much more powerful. Give your dream a title. This is immensely important as it can often provide a valuable clue as to what the dream is about. When choosing a title, you should look at the main symbol or theme of the dream. This is usually very apparent and doesn't need too much thought. A good tip is to write your title as though it were a newspaper headline. You'll notice that all the dreams, used as examples in this book, have a title. So, if you're unsure about what a title should look like, check these out.

As well as giving the dream a title, record the date of the dream, and the time if possible. You could also number the dreams consecutively. This facilitates easy cross-referencing as well as keeping a running total of the number of dreams recorded to date.

Be on the look out for puns, metaphors, parables and literal translations of clichés or feelings. Dreams are very adept at using these vehicles to tell their story and overlooking this can sometimes result in missing the point of the dream entirely. If you spot anything like this, make a brief note of it on the transcript.

After you've done all this, pinpoint anything in the dream that you can relate to your waking reality. Freud believed that every dream contained at least one element that had been experienced during the day prior to the dream. For instance; if you dream about a friend, who you haven't seen for years, the day after they telephone you, this may have a bearing on the interpretation.

If you start recording your dreams regularly, you will be surprised at how often you dream about such a friend a few days before they telephone you out of the blue! The apparent precognitive elements that appear in many dreams are a fascinating phenomenon but one that is too far reaching for discussion here. Incidences of this will undoubtedly become apparent to you as you build up your own dream journal.

Consider keeping your dreams on a computer; it has many advantages. It makes for easy editing and enables you to run searches for key words so you can check whether you've dreamt about a particular symbol or image previously. This helps tremendously in understanding your own personal dream symbolism and can provide the basis for compiling your own personal dream dictionary. It also makes it possible to track events in your life through the psyche and can give an excellent insight into how you are dealing with or have dealt with issues of importance.

If you don't have use of a personal computer, you will need to keep a written journal. The only drawback to this is that you won't have a search facility to enable you to quickly examine past dreams containing common symbols. Despite this, written journals have their advantages, especially if you use a loose ring binder and include a personal diary alongside your dream entries. This is what I used in the early days of recording my dreams. My personal diary was written on white paper and these sheets were placed next to the dreams of that day, which were written on brightly coloured paper, making them easy to tell apart. I still like to keep hard copies of my dream journals; they are fascinating to browse through in later years. At the end of each year, I take the print outs, (suitably illustrated), to a reputable book binder where they are professionally bound. They make an interesting addition to my bookshelves.

I've included two suggestions that you might like to use for the format of your Dream Journal. Once you start recording your dreams regularly you may want to devise a different format that better suits your needs and your dreams. These formats are presented only as suggestions; feel free to adapt them as you wish.

You can download free copies of these journal pages from www.uolearn.com.

Dream Journal

Date: .... Time: ....

Dream Story: ....
....
....
....
....
....
....
....
....
....
....

Title of the dream: ....
....

Prominent colour: ....
Prominent emotion: ....
Main character (self or other): ....
Man-made or natural environment: ....
Symbol or image that stood out: ....

Your feelings, thoughts and insights about the dream: ....
....
....
....
....
....

Date:	**Dreamwork**
	Feeling:
Title:	
	Background:
Dream story:	
	Theme:
	Generated questions:
	Symbols and associations:
	Dream message:
	Actions:

3.3: Sharing your dreams

Human beings, by and large, have experiences throughout their life that are similar to those of other human beings. And on a fundamental level we all experience the same emotions in response to the things that happen to us. This means that our dreams, which are forged from our emotions, can have important and deep meaning for other people. This, of course, is why story telling has been popular since time immemorial. And that's what dreams are; stories that we tell ourselves to try and make sense of our world and our experiences. Dream sharing was common in many societies and is, currently, undergoing something of a revival on the internet. Have a look on the internet for dreamwork groups and blogs.

If you're not part of a dream sharing network, it can sometimes be difficult to find a willing dream share partner. This doesn't stop you sharing your dreams with the world; the world just won't know that that's what you're doing! You can do this by incorporating your dreams into your life by acting on them whenever possible. For instance, if the dream seems to be suggesting that you contact a certain person; contact them.

If a dream animal appears to suggest that you need emulate its behaviour, go out and buy a physical representation of the animal and keep it wherever you feel you'll need to be reminded of its message or its character. Better still, if it's an animal you're in contact with, whether a pet or farm animal, or even a wild animal, spend some time quietly observing it. You might be surprised by what you learn. You could wear clothes of a particular colour on the day following a dream where that colour was prominent. Perhaps, you will chance on one of your dream images in your everyday reality.

I remember so well a dream I had in 1994 that featured a white candlestick decorated around the base with yellow flowers. On exploration of this symbol I came to realise that it had a very important message for me. A couple of days later I saw the exact same candlestick for sale in a shop window. I bought it and still have that candlestick with its pretty yellow flowers. Whenever I need to be reminded of its message, I take it from the cupboard, light a yellow candle, and spend a few minutes meditating on its message.

If you're lucky enough to find a partner to work with on your dreams, there must be an understanding between you from the start that neither of you will tell the other what their dreams mean. Discuss your dreams and devise ways of leading each other into a deeper understanding of the dream, but please don't impose your thoughts on each other. It will help to remember that an interpretation of someone else's dream says more about the interpreter than about the dreamer. I'm not saying that you should never share your opinion of someone else's dream; sometimes this can be helpful. Sometimes we overlook important aspects of our dreams for the simple reason that we're too close to them to notice, or we don't like what they might be inferring. A fresh eye can highlight such oversights and bring us to a much deeper understanding of ourselves and the dream. If we're happy to accept our own comfortable interpretation of a dream we may overlook a more significant interpretation because it doesn't conform to our own self-image. Those close to us sometimes see situations we are involved in more clearly than we see them ourselves.

To help your dreaming partner explore their dream in more depth, there follows a few suggestions about what you might like to ask them about their dream. These are not exhaustive and the questions you ask will depend on how the exploration of the dream develops. Use your imagination and LISTEN to what the dreamer says, picking up on any leads that present themselves during the exploration.

✓ How did you feel when you woke from the dream?

✓ When you think about the dream now, how does it make you feel?

✓ Did anything happen in the few days before the dream that you think may have caused the dream to occur?

✓ What title would you give this dream if it were a newspaper article?

✓ Do you recognise any of the people or elements from your waking life? If so, what associations/feelings do you have about them?

✓ Did any particular colour stand out in the dream?

✓ Can you describe the environment? (e.g. town, open country, indoors).

✓ What was the weather like in the dream?

✓ Is there anything in the dream that seems particularly bizarre or out of place?

✓ Is there anything you'd like to change in the dream? If so, why?

Once the dream has been explored in this way, you may feel you have a good idea what it means and be tempted to tell the dreamer what you think. If you really can't resist doing this, please ensure that you give your opinion in a totally safe, non-threatening way, by using the following method; a method suggested by Montague Ullman and widely used in group work. Suggested interpretations take the form of, "If this were my dream, I think it would mean............," or "If I'd had this dream, I would want to know ....."

Using this method, even a very ordinary dream can elicit many different interpretations depending on how the symbolism of the dream is explained. The method requires that other people apply the dream to their own lives and offer suggestions based on their own experiences. Providing it's understood that what's said is personal to the interpreter and not the dreamer, it can do no harm. The dreamer must, though, feel free to accept or reject anything that is said without feeling under pressure or worried that their response to suggestions may cause offence. It's important that those offering interpretations guard against imposing their ideas onto the dreamer. Sometimes it's easy to get carried away and, in the excitement of understanding, be too forceful. The whole point of this methodology is not to interpret the dream but to help the dreamer move closer into it and explore possibilities they might otherwise not have considered.

Exercise 4: If this were my dream.....

Read the following dream account and, using what you've learned so far about the language of dreams, write down what you think the dream might mean, assuming all the while that this is your dream.

Title: The Amethyst Plane Crash

It's a sunny day. I'm watching a plane flying overhead but there seems to be something wrong, it's bucking and buckling. I watch as it starts to lose height and eventually it crashes not far off. I'm covered in a shower of amethyst coloured glass. The glass looks so pretty, glinting and glittering in the sunlight as it falls to earth. I gather it up so no one will cut themselves on it.

Your ideas for interpreting this dream:

....

....

....

....

....

....

....

....

....

....

....

....

A plane crashing usually has disastrous consequences. This is a very common dream theme for people who are suffering intense anxiety coupled with a feeling that an emotional loss of some kind is imminent. This dream was taken from my own dream journal at a time when I was about to embark on a change of career and a change of residential area. I was under tremendous pressure and was unsure if I was making the right decision. Although this looks like a typical anxiety dream, do you think it's significant that I wasn't in the plane when it crashed? What about the amethyst coloured glass, described as glinting and glittering in the sunlight?

Dream symbols can be intensely complex and have meaning on many different levels and this is why, when attempting an in depth interpretation, it's necessary to look beyond the obvious. I saw the presence of amethyst as a positive sign and found it an empowering symbol that gave me strength to continue with my plans. How did you interpret this symbol?

Session 4:
Becoming More Aware

"A dream is a microscope through which we look at
the hidden occurrences in our soul." Erich Fromm

Session 4: Becoming More Aware

4.1: Overcoming censorship by the conscious ego

Ego was a term coined by Freud. He used it to describe the part of the psyche that is conscious, the part that most immediately controls thought and behaviour, and is most in touch with external reality. In our conscious mind we form an image of reality and of ourselves, as an individual, separate from other things. In other words, your ego is the part of you that you think of as "me", "I", "myself", a distinct entity, separate from the rest of the world. In this context, it's nothing to do with an inflated feeling of pride about ourselves. Our ego is what allows us to operate on a conscious level and be aware of what's going on around us. Without it we would not be able to make much sense of our life or our purpose. However, many people make the mistake of thinking they are, in their entirety, their ego when, in reality, the ego is only one part of the multi-faceted, complex human being that they are.

Dreams are not created by the conscious mind; they come from deep within the psyche. Dreams are the voice of your intuition. They originate from the you that is operating on a far more primitive level and are the result of emotions stirred by external and internal stimuli. This means that if something is affecting you, whether you are consciously aware of it or not, it can be woven into a dream story. Clearly, until you achieve conscious understanding, you won't be able to do anything about it. The problem with ego censorship is that it doesn't allow for a conscious understanding of something it doesn't want to acknowledge. This means that you may be totally unaware of behaviours and beliefs that are adversely affecting your life, and often your health, in ways you don't recognise. As Freud so eloquently explained,

"The ego is not master in its own house."

(Although it thinks it is!)

I need to warn you before we start, that it's not going to be easy. You'll need all the courage you can muster, and you'll need a sense of adventure, for your ego knows this is dangerous ground and it might get hurt. You need to commit to doing it anyway. So brace yourself dear reader.

The bottom line is that we can't fully understand what our dreams are telling us if we refuse to listen to some of the content. It's a psychological fact that we all, to a greater or lesser extent, censor what we hear, see and read. We dismiss many things that conflict with our belief systems. This is even more true for those things that conflict with our view of ourselves. Often we lie to ourselves to protect our self image and can become quite aggressive and defensive when our self-image is challenged by others. However, we are social animals and need to live productively amongst our fellow men if we are to survive. It's likely that the main function of our dreams is to help us to adapt, accept or change our relationships to obtain the best possible outcome for everyone.

If you are not aware of the possible ill effects of your ego holding sway over your life, you will likely fail to understand the signposts in some of your dreams that may be hinting at the damage you are doing to yourself and to your relationships. I want to stress at this point that dreams come in the service of health and wholeness. So whether they are highlighting our good, bad or indifferent traits, they are always striving for us to achieve a happy and fulfilling life.

Exercise 5: Obtaining feedback

Think about some of the arguments you've had in the past. Arguments where you felt very strongly that you were right and the other person was wrong. There may be such an argument going on at the present time, in which case this would be an excellent place to start. The protagonist may be a friend, a colleague, or even someone you dislike intensely. I'm going to request that you ask them to tell you something about yourself that they think you'd probably rather not know. I have to say, this exercise is more productive if it's someone you really don't get on with. The reason is that we often have a strong dislike for people who have personality traits that we ourselves have disowned, even though others may recognise exactly the same trait in us! To approach an enemy with such vulnerability is a tough call, so I'll understand if you shy away from that and choose a friend for this task. If it is a friend you choose, make sure they understand that you are asking them because you trust their judgement and that they are helping you to become more self aware.

Whomever you choose, it's important that you lay down the ground rules at the outset. Here are a few suggestions on how to handle this difficult exercise:

✓ Ask the person to promise to tell the truth and not censor what they say to spare your feelings.

✓ Tell them that you are totally committed to becoming more self aware and that this involves finding out how other people see you.

✓ Assure them that, whatever they say, you will take on board and not let it affect your relationship with them.

✓ Listen to what they have to say, without interrupting. When they are finished, thank them for their comments, assure them you will think very carefully about what they've said, and leave it at that. Don't get into a conversation about what's been said as this will often deteriorate into a case for the defence.

✓ Buy them a gift to say thank you; even if they are your worst enemy. They will have done you a great favour.

How you steer the conversation is up to you, but something along the lines of:

➢ Is there anything about me that you don't like very much?
➢ Is there anything about me that irritates you?
➢ Is there anything about me that you think I could improve?
➢ What do you like about me?

After you've gone through this process with one person, providing you feel you can cope with a second onslaught, try it again with another person.

It's also very useful to ask complete strangers about their first impressions of you on meeting. I recommend you do this as often as you can. A brief explanation about what you're hoping to achieve is usually enough to elicit a useful response. If you're uncomfortable with that, you can always say you're doing a bit of investigative journalism or conducting research into your own self-image. You'll find that most people are only too happy to help.

Ask questions such as:

➢ What were your first impressions of me?
➢ Overall, do I look happy or sad?
➢ Do I look like someone you would approach in the street?
➢ Has your initial impression changed since we've been chatting?

You might be very surprised by the feedback you receive and may find yourself wondering who's been looking back at you from the mirror all these years!

Record your findings in whatever format suits you best. A suggested format follows.

What are my positive character traits?

....
....
....
....

What's bad about these positives? (see following notes)

....
....
....
....

What are my negative character traits?

....
....
....
....

What's good about these negatives? (following notes)

....
....
....
....

What would I like to change?

....
....
....
....

What's bad about these positives?

Although there's not always a bad aspect to our positives, it's not always easy to see the bad if it's there. Bear in mind that the good things people see in you, could actually be something that's detrimental to yourself. For example, you may be told that you're always there for a friend when you're needed, or that you're very generous with your time and money. In this case, you could ask yourself whether you have enough time for yourself or enough money to treat yourself to a little luxury now and then. Are you sacrificing something, that's really important to you, in order to fulfil the expectations of others? You could also ask yourself how you felt when you heard the positive comments. Were you filled with pride? Did you feel like a really good person? Were you aglow to think that this person holds you in high regard? Then ask, is this why I do what I do? Perceiving yourself as a good person, a person who's well-liked, can strengthen your ego and bolster self esteem. It can mask the fact that, in other areas of your life, you feel like things are going wrong.

What's good about these negatives?

It's probably a little easier to recognise the good aspects of your negative traits. After all, if there was no pay off, you probably wouldn't do what you do. Once you've identified the good, or the pay off, ask yourself as honestly as you can, whether the benefit to you outweighs the detriment to others or even to yourself. Suppose someone tells you that you're miserly with your money, that they hate going out with you because you're always watching every penny. The positive aspect of this is that you probably spend less money than your friends and perhaps have more money to spend on the things that are important to you. It may mean that you're actively managing your money, which is good. If, on the other hand, you're holding onto your money whilst always allowing your friends to pay the bill, you probably need to acknowledge that this demonstrates selfishness and is unfair on your friends.

4.2: Ask your dreams

Now that you've gathered information about your conscious ego and how it's operating in everyday reality, we're going to look at the other side of the coin; the side without the face. We're going to look into the deep recesses of your mind to see what lies there, using an age old technique called dream incubation. It's a method by which we ask our subconscious a question and expect to have the answer revealed in a dream. It's a technique that was used for thousands of years throughout the ancient world. Indeed, incubating temples and shrines were built throughout Greece, Italy, and also the Middle East. There are many records that testify to its efficacy. Mainly used for healing purposes, it's a practice that works just as well for any problem. Ask your subconscious a question, with focussed intent and it will always respond. Not necessarily in the way you're expecting, but it will give an answer.

Exercise 6: Incubate a Dream

You're going to use some of the information gleaned from the research conducted in exercise 5 (obtaining feedback). Decide, from all the traits revealed by your research, which is the most important one. This will be the trait that you think is affecting your life more than all the others. It may be a positive or a negative trait. It doesn't matter which you choose as you can go back and use this method on all of them if you wish. The trait you choose will be the one you will work on for the next few days or weeks. Before you start, make sure you are quite clear about the character trait you've chosen; describe it in one sentence and write, very briefly, about the effect you think it's having on your life. There's space below for you to do this. As soon as you're sure you have absolute clarity, you can begin by incubating a dream. The instructions are on the following pages.

The character trait I'm going to work on is:

....

What affect does this trait currently have on my life?

....
....
....

Procedure for Dream Incubation

1. Make a commitment

Decide which night you will carry out the incubation. One to three days in the future usually works well. Note the date in your diary and make sure you leave the evening free to prepare yourself in relative isolation. You will also need to find some quiet time for introspection during the days leading up to the incubation.

If you have trouble remembering your dreams, make affirmations at regular intervals during this period. Positive affirmations of fact, such as, "I always remember my dreams," or "I do remember my dreams," are taken much more seriously by the subconscious than commands or affirmations of hope, such as "I will remember my dreams."

2. Set Your Intention

Intention is the key to the success of this procedure. You must **intend** to have a dream that will answer your question and this intention must be directed more by your subconscious than your conscious mind. By the time you incubate a dream, you should firmly believe that your subconscious is in possession of all relevant information and will give you a dream that will fully answer the question you pose.

3. Preparation

The preparation is an important aspect of the incubation and you must start this as soon as possible. It involves you seriously contemplating the purpose of the incubation. You must be absolutely clear about this and clear, too, about all the peripheral issues.

Give serious consideration to all the things you came up with in exercise 5 (obtaining feedback). Pay close attention to the immediate and foreseeable benefits/drawbacks of the character trait you are considering. Think about any possible actions you could take to either lessen a negative trait or develop a positive one. If you don't want to take any action, consider the fact that doing nothing is an important decision in itself. Make a list of the pros and cons of any action you might (or might not) take, or any decision you may make to instigate change. It's crucial that you examine some of the ways in which you may be possibly benefiting from your current behaviour. Honestly consider your readiness to let go of things that may be incompatible with your desire to become more self aware. If you can recognise these sources of resistance and still find yourself willing to let go of their benefits, you will open yourself to other ideas which may offer genuine possibilities for change.

Be very clear about what you hope to achieve from the incubation. It is this that will help you formulate a clear question that you can put to your dreaming mind. The clearer the question, the easier it will be to identify the answer in the dream. You're looking to find an effect and/or a solution to a specific character trait, so your affirmation should be along the lines of, "How does (this trait) affect my relationships/life/career?" or "Why do I need (this trait) to make me feel better about myself?"

If you feel you understand why you have a particular trait, and prefer to find a solution, try asking,

"How can I be less (negative trait)?" or

"What can I do about (this trait) to enhance my well being?"

As our dreams are in the business of resolving our everyday problems, it's likely that asking for a solution will produce a clearer response from your subconscious. Don't worry if the dream that comes seems totally unrelated to the question asked; chances are it is simply that your conscious ego cannot yet understand the response.

Think of some metaphors that aptly describe the trait you're considering. For instance; if you believe yourself to be clumsy, whether physically or emotionally, the metaphor *bull in a china shop* may be quite a good description of the havoc you think you sometimes cause. How about, *all fingers and thumbs*? People having problems with anger management might talk about *seeing red* or *doing battle*. All of these sayings conjure up visual images that could be used by your dreaming mind to answer your question. If you're in touch with your personal symbolism and the metaphors you use in everyday language, you will find it easier to understand the dream message.

Next, think about how you can approach the incubation in a way that reflects the inner process of self-guidance that will take place. How might you best enter into the spirit of the ritual during the few hours preceding the incubation? For instance; you may want to light candles, play music and perhaps spend some time in meditation. Bathing and grooming are traditionally symbolic acts of purification so a warm relaxing bath on the evening of the incubation will help promote a restful night. What will you wear for bed that night? You needn't wear nightclothes, why not wear something else? These are all personal matters left to your own discretion.

4. Create Your Dream Environment

Arrange your bedroom in a way that pleases you. Move the furniture round. Put your bed in a different place. The idea is to transform the space into your own symbolic sanctuary. Include objects with a spiritual significance or objects appertaining directly to the question you are asking.

Arrange your recording equipment within arms reach of the bed. Write the date of the incubation at the top of a piece of paper and write your question underneath. Put the paper under your pillow.

5. The Evening of the Incubation

Begin your incubation in the evening. To keep a clear and focused mind, I suggest you abstain from alcohol or caffeine during the day. Unplug telephones and switch off mobile phones. The world will not stop turning just because you opt out for a few hours. Settle yourself in a comfortable place with everything you have prepared around you. This initial period of incubation (lasting from one to four hours) is an opportunity for cathartic confession, prompting the activation prior to sleep of many of the ideas and feelings associated with your purpose.

Spend a few minutes in silence emptying your mind of all thoughts except the task in hand.

➢ Explain to yourself, out loud, the purpose of your incubation. Why are you doing this and what do you hope to achieve? Close your eyes and picture a scene that incorporates everything you've considered. If it helps, draw what you visualise. For example, if I want to try and be more patient, I might picture myself having a relaxed, friendly chat with someone who currently tries my patience to the limit.

➢ Imagine yourself having your answer. Savour what you wish to accomplish. Consider how accomplishing your purpose will put you in greater harmony with life and your highest ideals. Evaluate your readiness to make use of the fruits of your incubation. Commit yourself to be willing to act if action is suggested.

➢ Close your eyes and imagine a place of sanctity; a place that evokes a sense of reverence and feelings of safety. Somewhere you feel nurtured and comfortable. A place where you might go to think over an important problem. It may be a peaceful garden, or a secluded beach. A mountain retreat or a forest. Imagine it in every detail and imagine yourself in that space, how does it make you feel? You should feel serene and peaceful, and mildly excited at the prospect of receiving a dream that will help you in your self-development. If it's a forest, touch the trees and feel the earth beneath your feet. If it's a beach, go and have a swim in the sea. Feel the hot sand under your feet before you submerge yourself in the cool crystal water. Whatever environment you imagine will be your personal symbol of a special space. It's important that you imagine it in as much detail as you can.

➢ Now spend a few moments thinking about a person whom you would trust to give you good advice. Let's call this person your revered benefactor. It may be a person living or dead, for example your mother or friend, a religious leader, your dream messenger or your inner guide. It may not be a person at all, it may be an animal or a symbol. Build up a very clear mental image of this benefactor and place them in your place of sanctity. Watch how they interact with the environment and imagine them passing wise comment on your wish to become more aware. Believe in their power to see beyond the narrow limits of your own view point, and to speak with compassion and authority, offering insights and suggestions.

➢ Once you have this vision firmly implanted in your imagination, go and get ready for bed, performing any purification you have decided to do. All the while, practise holding the image of your special space and reminding yourself constantly of the question you want answering.

➢ When you get into bed, make yourself comfortable and go through a relaxation technique. A good one is adapted from the autogenic technique and is described below. Let go and trust in inspiration. Having worked hard on the present problem, you should now relax, releasing the problem to the subconscious, knowing that you will have your answer in the morning.

Relaxation technique

It may help to audio record this and play it back when you go to bed.

Lie down on your back and make yourself comfortable. Take a couple of deep breaths, holding the breath inside for as long as is comfortable for you. Return your breathing to normal and raise your arms up slightly. Notice how much effort it takes to resist the pull of gravity. Stretch them out, feeling the tension in the muscles. Now relax them as you slowly lower them back down. Experience the pleasure of letting go, of giving in to gravity. Push your legs down towards your toes. Feel the tension. Feel the lengthening. And then . . . . relax. Let the bed support you. Yours arms and legs feel heavy. Gravity is pulling them down into the bed. Enjoy the sensation of heaviness as you let go of all your problems and let the bed support you. You feel a tingling warmness in your arms and legs. You feel totally at peace. Think about your breathing. Follow the breath in and out. Think about how it's like the rolling motion of waves on the shore. As you inhale, think, "it breathes me", and then on the outward breath, think "relax". As you breathe out give a peaceful sigh of relief, relief that all chores are done for the day and now it's time to rest. Imagine that you're in a special, peaceful place. Allow the special, protective and comforting atmosphere to create a serene and calm feeling. Your arms and legs are heavy and warm. You have let go of your problem, yielding yourself to the support of the bed. You can hear your own voice telling you to relax with every peaceful sigh that marks your outward breath. You are safe within your peaceful place of healing. Imagine that your revered benefactor is approaching. Feel the special vibrations of their presence, and experience the confidence and optimism that is inspired in you. Let go with a peaceful sigh, trust in your intuition. Relinquish control of consciousness. You are falling asleep, prepared and willing for whatever might be given. Let go and sleep.

Record the Dream

Your dreaming mind is very fragile as you awaken, and can easily beat a retreat if interrupted by a blaring alarm clock, a restless partner or other distractions. Lie still as you replay the dream in your mind. If it's easier, start at the end and go through each scene until you reach the beginning. Stay in the same position you were in when you were dreaming. Don't move or even open your eyes until you are ready to record it.

Record the remembered dream(s) in as much detail as you can.

Acknowledge that the dream you may get may be nothing like you are expecting, so don't judge it. Keep an open mind and trust that your subconscious has come up with the answer, whether you initially understand it or not. If you've never incubated a dream before, it may be a good idea to repeat the incubation procedure for a few nights. You can also do this if the dream received on the first night is a very short dream that isn't going to provide much meat for an in depth analysis. Use your own judgement in this matter. We'll be talking about analysing a series of dreams later in the book.

In the next section, you will follow step by step instructions to analyse your incubated dream and, hopefully, bring new understanding to both the dream and yourself.

4.3: The dream ego

At the beginning of this session we talked about the conscious ego, the part of you that is at the centre of your waking reality. It's what gives you your unique identity, and it will do almost anything to protect its own self-image. However, is this the same "you" that is at the centre of all your dreams? You'll notice that the majority of them start with "I", "I was . . . " "I am . . . " "I went . . . ." etc.... but who exactly is this "I" in your dreams?

Imagine you're asleep and are dreaming that you're lazing around on a sun-drenched beach. Who exactly is the "you" who is enjoying this wonderful holiday for free? Clearly, it's not the "you" of your physical body, as this is immobilised on the bed. Is it the you who lives inside your head, the you who went to work today? What if this dreaming you starts to fly through the air like a bird? Does the you that went to work today, have wings? And for that matter, does the dreaming you even wonder why or how it's able to fly? Who exactly is this you we speak of? Looked at in this way, it's a bit of a conundrum! The dreaming you, is being dreamed by the person you think of as I. So let's turn our attention to that part of you that seems to be at the centre of all your dreams. To distinguish it from the conscious ego, let's call it the dream ego.

Most people have little understanding or knowledge of the dream ego. It operates in the dreamtime with seemingly complete autonomy and often seems to have an independent existence. If you thought about it, you may conclude that it exists in a world of fantasy and imagination, a world that's not real. Now let's turn this on its head and consider that your dream ego, if it knew of your existence, might view the you that's reading this book in the same way! The dream ego believes itself to be just as "real" as your waking consciousness believes itself to be real. We might say that the dream ego isn't "real" because it doesn't conduct, what we call, reality testing. If it did, you (it) would realise you were dreaming, and you would either wake up or experience the wonder of a lucid dream. It accepts everything that happens in the dream as if it were normal and "real", no matter how bizarre or unlikely. Have you ever conducted a reality test as you go about your daily business?

During normal, daily routines like walking down the street or making a cup of tea, have you ever asked yourself, is what I'm seeing and doing, actually real? Do you just accept that, what you call your everyday reality is the real world? Think about it, isn't this just what your dream ego does? It's almost as though the dream ego has a separate existence in a separate reality and (usually) has no idea that another reality, the everyday world, exists. Do we really know, with one hundred percent certainty, which of these existences is "real"? There are those who would say that reality is what goes on inside our head, not what is outside. Others may say the only reality is what's going on at the molecular or atomic level. At that level, a pavement is not a pavement at all, it's mainly empty space. The only truth of which we can be certain is that our personal reality is dependent on how we choose to interpret what's out there, the things that we recognise as being non-self. This interpretation is experienced in our dreams by our dream ego.

Just as the conscious ego is the most consistent thing in our everyday world, the dream ego is the most consistent thing in our dreaming life. It's present in almost every dream and seems to be a fair representation of ourselves, in that, on the whole, it seems to act with the same values. By tracking its activities we can monitor the development and changes that occur in its behaviour and mode of thinking and these changes can be translated into changes occurring at the conscious ego level. More importantly, by tracking the dream ego, we can recognise what we need to change in the life or behaviour of our conscious ego and take conscious action to bring this into our everyday reality. The dream ego, if you like, is the reflection that Alice sees as she gazes into the looking glass. It tells us the truth of what we are and what we feel and seems to operate at an impartial level, paying no heed to the demands of our self image. Our conscious ego on the other hand finds impartiality difficult, to such an extent that it does not always recognise its own blind spots or its short-comings.

4.4: Analysing a dream

Let's now turn this knowledge to practical use. There follows a method of dream analysis that will enable you to get to know your dream ego, which is essentially the unconscious you and who actually exerts a lot of subliminal power over the conscious you. If you examine your dream ego carefully, and get to know it in all its aspects, you'll find the essence of your being. For this method to be effective, you must view your dream ego as you would a stranger, someone who sometimes behaves in very different ways to you. This stranger experiences the world in terms of feeling; feelings that the conscious "you" may not immediately recognise. Compare yourself to this person in the dream. How are you the same? How are you different? Is this person in the dream some hidden part of you - some part you wish for, need or fear?

The method we're going to use is based on a technique proposed by Strephon Kaplan-Williams, who founded the Jungian-Senoi Institute for Dreamwork in 1977. The main thrust of his method is in what he calls *objectifying the dream* and then evaluating the dream ego and following its progress over time. To objectify the dream it's necessary to remove yourself entirely from your personal connection to the dream. You must try not to identify or make associations with the dream images. The dream ego (or Drego as Strephon fondly called it) is seen as representing the viewpoint of the real you or core self, considered by Strephon to be the source of all dreams. Think of it in terms of the unconscious self.

By examining the dream as if it were a story told by a complete stranger, it is possible to uncover aspects of our true nature. What is uncovered is sometimes at odds with the viewpoint of the conscious ego. By examining the way the dream ego conducts itself, and deals with problems and situations, the conscious ego can bring those principles into its own reality. It gives the opportunity to live a life that is more in accord with your true self. The method given here is an adaptation of Strephon's methodology. You will use this method to analyse your incubated dream from exercise 6.

Method for analysing a dream

1. Record the dream as completely as you can. Use third person (he/she/they) and the present tense. (Normally you'd record your dreams in the first person I/me.)

2. Make a list of the events and developments in the dream. .

3. List and evaluate the actions and reactions of the dream ego

4. Make note of any contradictions or similarities in the dream action or symbols.

5. List and evaluate the things the dream ego could have done, but didn't.

6. List the attitudes of the dream ego that lie behind its actions, reactions and non-actions.

7. What do you think are the issues being dealt with by the dream ego in this dream? There will almost always be some sort of conflict within the dream. Identification of the conflict will highlight the issues involved.

8. Is the dream ego effective in dealing with, or resolving, the dream issues identified in 7?

9. Make a simple list of sequences and developments in the dream in terms of cause and effect. For example: The dream ego did this, causing that to happen.

10. Apply what you've discovered to your waking life. Can you see any parallels in terms of life issues, attitudes, actions and non-actions?

11. Pick a character or symbol from the dream that has the most energy – positive or negative. Write down five questions that you would like to ask of this character or symbol.

12. Put yourself back into the dream at the point where you would have been in a position to ask these questions. This will require you to be in a relaxed, meditative state. Keep the character or symbol in your mind's eye and go through the questions you have prepared. Listen to the answers given and write down **everything** that occurs to you. As you do this, other questions may arise. Feel free to ask as many questions as you like. Keep on until the flow stops or you find you have discovered a resolution to the issue(s) in question.

13. Having got this far, you should by now have a pretty good idea as to what action you feel your dream ego should have taken and didn't. Decide what action you would like to try out.

14. Make a note of the habits or behaviours you have discovered through studying your dream ego. Make a conscious resolution to either discard these or work at developing them, whichever is appropriate.

15. Make a list of new behaviours and principles that you will live by from now on.

16. Decide on some definite course of action that will reinforce what you've written down in 13 and 14. Give yourself a reasonable time limit and promise yourself that you will take this action within that time.

Following is an example to show how this method can be used. At the end of the section, I will ask you to use the same method to analyse your dream from exercise 6 (incubate a dream), bearing in mind what you have learned in exercise 5 (obtaining feedback).

Example dream analysis

The Dreamer is a divorced man in his early 50s. Despite having had a successful career, he still feels a lack of confidence in his own abilities and judges himself to have low self-esteem.

Step 1: The Dream recorded by the dreamer in the third person.

Dream title: Cormorant on the Crag

The DE (dream ego) is on a ramble with lots of other people. He's way ahead and is walking with someone else. He's carrying a toy car. They walk up a lane towards open moorland and his companion suggests that they stop when they get near the top because they're not sure where they're going. DE parks his toy car up in a little lay by. The open moorland stretches out before him. He looks back down the hill and sees the rest of the group turning off the lane onto a footpath on their left. It runs through the valley. DE hurries back down to join them and tags on at the back. A very small woman approaches him. DE has his mobile phone in his right hand and the woman grabs that hand to chastise DE and tell him where he went wrong on the walk. She's like a dog, snapping at DE and won't let go. DE says, very aggressively, "Will you get off me?" but the woman is still shouting and hanging on to him. DE decides to ignore her and turns his head away to the left. He says, under his breath in exasperation, "Oh, go away." DE looks up to a high craggy peak on his left. On the top sits a huge, black bird. He thinks it's a cormorant but it actually looks like a huge stork. It's so high up it must be able to see everything. The woman is still snapping at DE and DE senses a great deal of evil emanating from her. DE needs to get away. He turns back to the woman and asks, very calmly, why she's behaving in this way. The woman says she doesn't like DE. DE wants to know why. The woman doesn't answer.

Step 2: List of events and developments

Dream Ego (DE) walks up a lane, going up hill.

The companion suggests they wait for the others to catch up.

DE parks his (toy) car in a lay-by.

The group turn onto another path.

DE hurries back down the hill to join them.

DE re-joins the others at the back.

A woman grabs DE's arm, shouting at him, telling DE where and why he went wrong.

DE aggressively tells her "get off me."

The woman won't let go.

DE turns away, trying to ignore her.

DE sees a cormorant that looks like a stork, perched high on a craggy peak.

DE feels the need to get away from the "evil" woman and tries another tactic.

DE asks the woman why she's shouting at him.

Woman says she doesn't like DE but won't tell him why.

Step 3:

Dream Ego Actions/ Reactions/Non-action	Evaluation
Walking up hill.	Takes effort but good exercise
Walking in front, striding ahead.	Want to walk at own pace. Others are lagging behind – the companion (the moderating side of the personality?) suggests they wait for them.
Parks up the toy car.	The dreamer had a fascination for toy cars as a child.
They wait for the others to catch up.	DE assumes it has gone the wrong way when it sees the others turn onto a different path.
They return to the group.	Brought back into line. Back-tracking. Held back.
DE feels trapped when the aggressive woman grabs the hand holding the mobile phone.	The mobile phone is the means by which the DE keeps in touch with friends, it's a communication device, but DE doesn't want to communicate with the aggressive woman.
DE wants to escape the grip of the aggressive woman but takes no decisive action.	DE turns away, wants to avoid confrontation.
DE sees and acknowledges the beauty and peace of the cormorant.	The bird is high up; it must be able to see all over the countryside. It is jet black like a cormorant, and yet has the shape of a stork; which is white.
DE tries to communicate with the aggressive woman in a calm manner.	The aggressive woman wants only to tell the DE about its faults.

Step 4: Contradictions and similarities

DE forging ahead, others lagging behind.

Communication – DE is carrying a mobile phone and the aggressive woman is communicating her anger towards DE.

Black bird; colour of a Cormorant, shape of a stork – cormorants are black, storks are white.

Cormorants live by the sea, they do not perch on high inland crags.

Step 5: Dream ego "could have done"

➢ Carried on walking alone over the moorland, leaving the group behind

➢ Made his toy car normal size and driven away over the moor

➢ Ask politely that the aggressive woman calm down

➢ Physically make the aggressive woman let go of him

➢ Returned to the top of the hill and carried on alone

➢ Flown up to the crag to sit with the cormorant and watch the scene from that perspective.

Step 6: What are the dream ego's attitudes shown by these actions/reactions/non-actions?

➢ The need to comply and be one of the crowd – even if it means going back (being held back) and re-tracing its steps.

➢ The need to exercise caution whilst walking in unknown territory; there's safety in numbers.

➢ Doesn't want any hassle. Doesn't want confrontation.

➢ Messages are conveyed to us from the natural world

➢ Altercations need to be resolved

➢ Keep away from anything perceived as being evil

Step 7: What are the issues that the Dream Ego is dealing with?

There is a conflict between wanting to be independent and go its own way at a pace that suits it (which is faster than most other people) versus wanting to have a group identity and feel part of that group. However, the DE recognises that conformity means compliance, not standing out from the crowd, being like everyone else; otherwise he will be resented and reprimanded. The toy car may suggest that the DE is playing with the possibility of breaking free of constraints. Testing the ground; seeing what will happen. It might also suggest a lack of personal power. The DE also is trying out various ways he can deal with the conflicts that may arise as a result of his independence.

Step 8: What is the dream ego's effectiveness in dealing with or resolving these issues?

The Dream Ego has complied with the wishes of the crowd but is faced with a barrage of abuse for forging ahead and not staying with the group. The DE tries different strategies to deal with the abusive woman; initially trying to combat aggression with aggression. It doesn't work, so he tries the polar opposite to aggression by ignoring her. It still doesn't work. Finally he confronts the woman directly in a calm, assertive manner and is given the reason for the abuse – the woman doesn't like him. This is an important disclosure for it suggests that whatever the DE does or doesn't do, the woman will find cause to be abusive.

Step 9: Dream cause and effect

DE gets ahead and finds himself alone.

The group turn away onto a less challenging route so DE returns to them.

DE is reprimanded for having rushed on ahead. DE deals with the aggression in an aggressive manner and then in a dismissive manner – but the woman has DE in her grip.

DE sees the bird on the crag, causing him to try a different, more mature, approach.

Step 10: Parallels to waking life issue

The dreamer recognises that the dream is addressing very important issues in his life. He's an avid walker and is always found right at the front of his walking group. This is reflected in his everyday life as he always forges ahead in everything he does. He rarely stands still in life, keeping lots of projects on the go at the same time and on constant look out for the next challenge. He has always had an insatiable thirst for knowledge and has an impressive collection of books. He excels academically but as a child was scorned for being a know it all. He's achieved a great deal more than most people and yet, if asked, will say he's achieved little. He admits that often he feels lonely, especially since his marriage break-up, and also feels estranged from his parents and siblings. He feels he lacks pride in his achievements because his family doesn't seem to value them.

Despite never having had problems making close friendships, he's a bit of a loner and values his own space. Being a person of action, he doesn't work very well in a team if his enthusiasm for getting things done is restrained. He admits that he has a tendency to walk away from relationships that have become difficult rather than face the hassle of trying to sort things out.

Step 11: The symbol with the most energy

The small, aggressive woman.

The Dreamer's five questions for her:

➢ Why don't you like me?

➢ Who are you?

➢ Where were you born?

➢ How old are you?

➢ What can I do to make you like me?

Step 12: The answer

Why don't you like me? – You think you're so good, better than the rest of us. You rush up the hill, looking down on us, while we try and catch up. You think you're always right – well, hey, not this time. You went the wrong way. If you hadn't rushed on ahead, you wouldn't have made a mistake would you? You should learn from this. In future, you stay with us and don't go wandering off.

Who are you? – Someone who knows you well, believe you me. Better than you know yourself. I know what's best for you. You will listen to me and do as I say in future.

Where were you born? – Inside you. (Laughs). I've always been here. And you know it.

How old are you? A lot older than you are. I'm your elder and better. Just remember that.

What can I do to make you like me? Fail! Fall flat on your face! Be a victim like the rest of us!

Step 13: The action I would like to try that my dream Ego did not do

The Dreamer said he would like to walk on alone, over the moorland; leave the group behind. Set out on an adventure, cover new ground and go into uncharted territory. He felt there was nothing to fear in the dream except the angry woman.

Step 14: Habits and behaviours discovered

The dreamer concluded that he has a deep need to be accepted by the group, a need that was also apparent in his childhood. He also recognises that he values his independence and that these two aspects of his character are somewhat conflicting. He has tried all his life to conform to what is expected of him but his temperament is such that he cannot comply willingly nor graciously with a group mind that limits him. This means that, despite his best efforts, he has never felt fully accepted into any group. The dream showed him that to achieve acceptance he must compromise and submit to the will of those who believe they know better. The dream also tells him that hassle and confrontation cannot be avoided if he chooses to travel a different path to everyone else and that he must learn to deal with this in a more informed, mature way. There have been family problems around this issue for most of his life and he acknowledged that these problems had got worse in the past few years, especially since his marriage break-up.

Step 15: New behaviours and principles

The dreamer decided it was time for him to stop worrying about not complying with others' expectations of him. These were reflecting someone else's values and beliefs, not his own. He resolved to stop feeling guilty about his independence and celebrate his achievements and his uniqueness.

He suggested that perhaps he might try communicating his feelings to those who seem to disapprove of him, even if this means a confrontation. If those people are not willing to respect who he is and be happy about his independence and achievements, then they must be left behind.

Step 16: Action to be taken

The dreamer decided to temporarily withdraw from people and situations whom he felt disapproved of his independence. He also resolved to try and improve relations with a significant family member from whom there had been constant disapproval, by responding in a more positive way. He decided that if attempts to repair this relationship failed, then he would remove himself completely from that sphere of influence as he now recognised that it had been a destructive influence in his life. The dreamer also acknowledged that, despite his apparent independence, his feelings of insecurity had meant that he'd never had the courage to holiday alone and had never been away from home for more than a week in thirty years. A short while after the dream, he made plans to rectify this. The following summer, he spent five weeks camping and trekking round the Californian National Parks, alone, and had a wonderful time.

Outcome

The dreamer reported later that he had become more self-accepting and was now proud of his achievements. It's hard to break the habit of a lifetime but he did become less reliant on the approval of others and forged ahead with radical life changes. In addition, he sought out friends who were more supportive of his undertakings and withdrew from those who only sought to control.

The Author's additional notes on the dream

The angry woman is a classic example of a saboteur; a part of the psyche that is continually trying to undermine confidence in oneself and destroy all attempts at growth. A saboteur keeps us locked in internal conflict, often presenting as the voice of reason and moderation, as in the case of the companion in this dream, or in the role of disapproving parent, as in the angry woman. Saboteurs are often borne in our childhood. That are often instigated by well meaning parents who feared for our safety; "No you can't cross the road on your own." "No you can't stay out until 9pm." "Be careful, the world is a dangerous place." You get the picture. The problems caused by the saboteur can be compounded when people continue to treat us in this way because it taps into the same patterns that accumulated when we were children, and it elicits the same, often childish, response from us. As adults, the threat of direct punishment for disobeying our elders is removed, being replaced by more subtle punishments. These take the form, more often than not, of emotional disapproval stemming from unreasonable jealousies that further undermine our efforts to develop and grow. The secret is to recognise this and begin to react as an adult and not as a child. This dream showed these truths to the dreamer in a beautifully eloquent way and you can see that step 12 was particularly enlightening, especially the last question which directly tapped in to the childhood accusations of being a know it all.

The appearance of the bird on the high crag was the cue to the dream ego to look at the problem more objectively; from a higher perspective. The contradiction in colour, black cormorant but looking like a stork, which is white, suggests there is great clarity to be gained by looking at the situation from a distance. The dreamer also commented that he associates storks with new birth, and so this suggests a new way of looking at an old problem. The fact that the cormorant, a sea bird, is seen inland may also suggest that this is a difficult area for the dreamer. However, following the appearance of the bird, the dream ego confronts the saboteur in a calm, mature way and, although the answer he gets seems unsatisfactory, it is actually immensely revealing. The saboteur doesn't like him, purely and simply because he is who he is. When the dreamer acknowledges that he's proud of who he is his saboteur will be silenced. Sometimes this can take many years and many dreams.

Exercise 7: An in-depth dream analysis

Taking the dream from exercise 6 (Incubate a dream), use the method described above to analyse it. Take your time. This process cannot be rushed and the most important insights often come after many days or weeks of contemplation. Make detailed notes during your analysis. Include drawings and sketches to illustrate the dream and your findings. Afterwards write a brief note in the box below, describing what you have learned about yourself, and what action you intend taking, as a result of this first step into dreaming yourself aware. Other ideas may arise as you continue to work on the dream, months or even years later. Remember, the whole point of dream work is not to interpret a dream per se, but to increase self-knowledge so that you are empowered to take action in your waking life; action that will improve the quality of your life and bring you closer to the ultimate goal of self-realisation.

What I've learned about myself:

....
....
....
....
....
....
....
....
....
....

The action I will take is:

....
....
....
....
....
....

Having gone through this process with one dream, look for changes in the behaviour of your dream ego in any new dreams that seem to be dealing with the same, or similar, issues. If you see a development, give yourself a pat on the back; you have undergone a period of growth. I recommend you come back to this exercise time and again, working on other issues from exercise 5 (feedback).

Important reminder

Dream interpretation without action is like buying a map and never setting foot outside your front door.

Notes

Session 5:
Working with
your Dreams

"In dreams, we enter into a sea
of possibilities and potentials" Joan Harthan

Session 5: Working with your Dreams

I hope you enjoyed using the technique given in the last session and, more importantly, I hope you gained a lot of useful insights. Clearly it's not practicable to use this lengthy technique on all your dreams, there are other things in life that demand our attention besides our dreams! However, dream analysis as a tool for self-knowledge is only really useful if it is ongoing. Recognising that most people don't have time to analyse every dream in such depth, I've presented here a selection of useful techniques that take less time. These techniques will also be useful in identifying those dreams that would benefit from a more in depth analysis. Use them and change them in whatever way suits your purpose, but always resolve to take some action, no matter how small. By doing this, you will be sending a very powerful message to your subconscious that you are honouring the dreams it produces. As a reward, your subconscious will produce more interesting and purposeful dreams.

5.1: Mapping a dream

In the last section we talked at length about ego censorship and the way in which our conscious ego can sometimes deny, or fail to see, important messages in our dreams. The effects of this censorship mustn't be underestimated as it can sometimes lead to protracted and painful life experiences. The dream mapping technique is useful for by-passing the censorship effect as it gets right to the emotional heart of the dream without any analytical input. It uses colour and shape, rather than the actual images or symbols that make up the dream and gives the opportunity to use visual forms for feelings and emotions that are sometimes too nebulous to recognise. It's more effective if you use it on dreams that left a deep impression or were particularly vivid.
In session 2, exercise 3 you discovered your own personal associations to different colours and this discovery can now be put to good use. In addition, I want you to think about shape and its emotional connotations.

In 2001, Ramachandra, a neurologist best known for his work in the fields of behavioural neurology and psychophysics, famously repeated Köhler's earlier experiments to try and throw some light on the evolution of language. He took two different shapes, one spiky and jagged, and the other rounded and curvy. He asked people which was the "kiki" and which was the "bouba". Ninety eight percent of people chose the bouba as the soft shape, and the kiki as the spiky shape. More recent research by Daphne Maurer has shown that even children as young as two and a half years old show this effect. It's this inherent human capability to associate colour and shape with emotion that we'll be using here. The method works best on dreams that left you feeling uncomfortable. A dream that worried you or left you with a feeling that something wasn't quite right is ideal material. It's also a very useful technique to use with children who have been disturbed by a nightmare. It can quickly and safely reduce their fear by giving them the power to change whatever was frightening them, into something harmless or even humorous.

How to map a dream

A map of a dream is a picture that shows the flow of the story and feel of your dream without necessarily being the scenes of the dream.

Gather together anything you can lay your hands on; things that you can use to cut, paste, model or draw. This may include coloured pencils and crayons, paints, brightly coloured paper or fabric. You will also need plain paper. Take a few moments recalling the dream you're going to work on. Concentrate on the feeling it gives you, deepen it, get right into it. What are the emotions you experience as you examine each detail of the dream? Really feel it. Immerse yourself in it. Meditate on it. For instance, you may feel fear or panic as you hide from a menacing dream character. What colour or shape best represents this feeling? Perhaps the colour red moulded into a spiky, rough textured shape? Or perhaps the fear makes you feel like you can't breathe. Perhaps you associate this with drowning, in which case you might want to portray it as a deep, dark blue colour with barely seen shadows lurking in it. What about your pursuer? Is he/she/it angry, vengeful or hungry? How can you portray those emotions and whereabouts on your map will you place the representation?

Give your map a three-dimensional feel. Consider how the shapes, colours and arrangements relate to each other. As you work on your picture, always be aware of how the dream is relating to how you feel about your life right now. What do you think the dream might have been about?

Once completed, examine your work. Stand back from it and feel what it's trying to say to you. If it could talk, what would it say? Now consider which parts are lacking something. Do you want to add something else that doesn't seem related to the dream? Do you want to change some aspect of your map to improve it, make it better; make you feel better about it? You can either make the changes on your existing picture or start afresh on a completely new piece of paper. Give yourself free rein to do as you please. Once you are happy with the finished product, think carefully about any changes you have made and how they might relate to your life. Can you translate these changes into action you could take in your life to make your current situation more like the revised dream map and less like the original? For instance, if the dream made you feel like you couldn't breathe, what is it in your life at the moment that makes you feel like that? If you'd denoted this feeling by dark blue and you changed this to a bright, airy pale blue, or sunlight yellow, think what action you could take in your everyday life to give you more air and/or sunshine, either metaphorically or physically. Are these changes feasible? How would you implement them?

Example of mapping a dream

This dream is taken from my own dream journal. As you read the dream, note the similarities to the recurring childhood dream I talked about in the introduction. The dream I recount here is a wonderful example of how some images endure in our psyche throughout our whole life and, once understood, can be used to better understand the present. In this case, the dream was prompted by the need to break free of the limitations and constraints that I was unconsciously placing on myself.

Dream Title: *The baby who tries to fly*

I'm walking down a sloping road that is covered in ice. There's a couple in front of me with a very young baby. The baby is tiny, only about 10 to 15 centimeters long, and is crawling on the road in front of the couple. The ice on the road is starting to melt, so bare patches of road are showing through. The baby picks up speed and starts scooting down the road, incredibly fast. It isn't slipping because it seems to be taking care to only touch the road that's ice free. I watch in awe as it tries to fly. It actually succeeds in taking off and flies for a few seconds, flapping its arms as if they were wings. I'm astounded and say to the person with me, "Look at that, it's amazing! It's just like a bird." The mother of the baby overhears me. She stops and waits until I've caught up. She looks very cross and starts chastising me, "Do you mind not saying that. If the baby hears you, it will think it is a bird and will carry on behaving like that." I apologise. I shouldn't have said anything. I was out of order and have no business interfering with her parenting.

You can see my map of this dream in figure 1 (you can see these figures in colour at www.uolearn.com). The dream left me with a feeling of frustration and annoyance at myself for apologising for my comments to the mother of the baby. The baby is trying to do something amazing and it should be encouraged. If it wants to be a bird, let it try. If it fails, it can try again, and again. Better to have tried and failed than to live in the grey world of can't do, better not and too risky. I'm reminded of Jonathan Seagull. A parent has no right to censor a child's dreams. In my map I represent the mother as a large, spiky rectangular bloc. This is the self-critical part of me, the part that thinks it knows better; my saboteur. It is the authoritarian, parental voice that tells me not to aim above my station. It's the part of me that won't allow the seeds of new growth to break through the ceiling of limitation. Notice how the spiky block extends beyond this ceiling. It knows what lies beyond but chooses to instil fear into the baby. How else can it keep control over the freedom-loving, rebelliousness?

The soft, round shapes within the block are coloured pink to represent the parental love that fears for my safety, the part that fears disappointment, failure and rejection. These are the shapes that give rise to the lightning bolts and the flowers, for love both hurts us and cherishes us. Below the barrier of limitation there is a sombre world of grey and black, interspersed with patches of ice. Here I've placed myself as the tiny baby, glowing yellow. Trying to fly, trying to get out and trying to break free. Face down, about to drown in a sea of grey. Above the barrier it is night-time. A pale crescent moon gives little light, just like the future; not enough light to see things clearly. I have no way of knowing what lies beyond the barrier.

It was very easy to make changes to this dream map. The baby, as an aspect of me, is an amalgamation of the child within and the part of me that is eager to push forward with a new phase of growth in my life. It clearly wants to fly and so my revised map (figure 2) allows it to do just that. The baby, now grown and with fully functional wings, explodes through the barrier, leaving behind the grey depths of self-doubt. We see it soaring up like a bird into a landscape of rolling green hills, blue sky and brilliant sunshine. What powerful imagery with which to encourage myself to step out into the unknown and try something new!

Figure 1: the original dream (see www.uolearn.com for the colour version)

Figure 2: the new picture (see www.uolearn.com for the colour version)

5.2: Association

This method makes use of associations to the ideas and images in dreams to unlock their symbolic meaning. Both Freud and Jung used it extensively. Jung described the technique as a spontaneous flow of interconnected thoughts and images around a specific idea, often determined by unconscious connections. Freud, in his use of free association, would allow his clients to follow their associations to exhaustion. Unlike Freud, Jung ensured that he continually brought his client back to the dream symbol rather than allowing them to lose sight of it and thus become lost in free associations, which in the end may have nothing to do with the dream meaning. He felt that exploring images to exhaustion, as Freud did, could result in confusion and also an interpretation that is so far removed from the dream as to be pure conjecture. He believed that the symbol itself held the key, and the mind must not be allowed to sidetrack in an effort to avoid confrontation with the deep issue that the symbol represented;

> "I work around the dream picture and disregard every attempt that the dreamer makes to break away from it."

It's important to remember that feelings about words or images are just as important as concrete associations and so you must write down the first thing that comes into your mind, e.g. mattress on the floor may prompt words like dirty, poverty or squatters which may then lead to feelings of disgust or pity.

Method for associating images and symbols

Note down the key images and symbols from the dream on a piece of paper; writing each one at the top of its own column. Write the associated words or feelings underneath the relevant column heading. These notes can be used to further amplify the dream meaning later. If you are not sure which components of the dream story constitute the symbols, they are usually identifiable as the nouns (naming words). Starting with the first symbol write down the associations, (feelings or images), that spring to your mind directly from that particular word. It doesn't have to be just one word; it can be all the feelings or emotions associated with a word or concept.

Example of association

Dream Title: The hibernating Dalek

I was faced with a Dalek*; obviously it was a lot stronger than me and I couldn't overcome it but then suddenly it went into a cupboard and became quiescent. Someone thought I'd made it go quiet but I said it had chosen to do that; it must have gone into hibernation.

Dalek	Cupboard	Hibernation
Scared me as child	Put things away	Go to sleep for a while
Robotic	Tidy up	Don't eat
Unfeeling	Out of sight	State of suspended animation
Hard metal		Not fully alive
Not human, alien		Will wake up eventually
Destroyer		

*(A sinister very powerful creature from Doctor Who that can exterminate people with a ray gun.)

The dreamer had been off work for a few months with work-related stress and had this dream two weeks after returning to work. The comments in the table show clearly how the dreamer is dealing with this situation. The Dalek is how his psyche is representing his feelings about his work/employer – feelings of powerlessness along with the fear that it could destroy him. To return to work he had to push these feelings away, they are still there but have temporarily been put into hibernation. In his waking reality, the dreamer needs to decide how he will deal with this Dalek. Should he pull it out of the cupboard and befriend it? Should he try and fight it? Or should he accept that he is powerless against it and remove himself from harm's way? Alternatively he could do nothing; though if this is his decision, he must know that the Dalek will wake up from its hibernation eventually, perhaps with renewed energy.

Action taken:
The dreamer decided to leave the job.

5.3: Verbal analysis, doing and describing (verbs, adverbs and adjectives)

The Association technique, described above, looks at the symbols and images; these are mainly the nouns, the things that we can see and describe easily. A different technique is to focus on the verbs, adverbs and adjectives that we've used to record the dream. This approach quickly draws out the emotional content of a dream and is useful for ascertaining the situation that gave rise to the dream.

What are verbs, adverbs and adjectives?

Verbs are the "doing" words that convey the action, or state of being. They can be past, present or future tense. For example:

I **ran** to the forest. (past)

I **feel** warm. (present)

I **will leave** soon. (future)

Adverbs are used to modify a verb, an adjective or another adverb. They are added to another word to express some modification of the meaning or an accompanying circumstance. For example:

I spoke **loudly**. (modifies the verb spoke)

I was **very** cross with him. (modifies the adjective cross)

I was speaking **too** quickly. (modifies the adverb quickly)

Adjectives are descriptive words that qualify a noun (person, place, object or idea) or pronoun (he, she, her, him etc...). It describes size, colour, how many, which one, whose or what kind. For example:

The **old** woman stroked a **black** cat as she pointed her **bony** finger at the **little** girl.

Here is an example of how all these are included in one sentence:

I **was running** (verb) **away from** (adverb) a **huge** (adjective) tiger.

Method for verbal analysis

Two pens of different colours will be useful; highlighter pens are ideal.

In your dream notes (or a copy) highlight or underline what you feel are the most important verbs and accompanying adverbs in one colour, and all the adjectives and accompanying adverbs in a different colour. Make two lists of all the highlighted words and see if you can make any connection with something happening in your life at the moment. For instance; if you're running away from something in your dream, is there something you are running away from in real life, or perhaps something that you feel you ought to run away from?

By examining the actions and emotional content of the dream, its true meaning is less vulnerable to self-deception and the truth can often be revealed with very little effort. The success of this technique, however, will depend on the nature of the dream.

If you need further insight you can move onto the nouns (characters, symbols and images) connected to those actions or feelings.

Example of verbal analysis

Dream Title: Long wait in the restaurant

I'd gone out for a meal with my children. We'd left home thinking the restaurant was quite close but we had quite a long journey to get to it. When we arrive, (around 9pm), it is very busy. It's a small, family run place. We're still sitting at the dining table, not having been served, at 10.30pm. We haven't even ordered. I'm getting quite cross, I'm so hungry.

Verbs/Adverbs	Adjectives/Adverbs
Gone out	Long (journey)
Left home	Very busy
Arrive	Small, family-run
Still sitting	(place)
Haven't ordered	
Quite cross	
Hungry	

As soon as the dreamer had listed these words it was apparent to her that they were describing how she felt about her job. She had moved away from her hometown (gone out) to take up a new appointment and had worked extremely hard to quickly become a key member of staff in a small organization that had a very supportive, family atmosphere. Although her input was recognised and valued, the rewards had been slow in coming. So the dream was illustrating her feelings about this situation. She had left home, arrived in a new job, been very busy (to the exclusion of a social life) for a long time and yet was still sitting, waiting for her rewards. She also admitted to feeling quite cross about it. She was hungry for the financial rewards that she felt were due her.

Action

The Dreamer resolved to approach her boss and ask for an increase in her pay. If it was refused, she would apply for other, more rewarding, positions.

5.4: Theme, Affect, Question, Outcome

This method attempts to identify the life issue or situation that gave rise to the dream. Dream themes can reflect major issues, or may simply be expressing personal characteristics, attitudes or behaviour. Intensive work on a dream theme can help you gain a better understanding, not only of the personal meaning of a dream and what is important to you at the time, but also of yourself and how you really feel about certain situations in your life. This method will also allow you to identify a desired outcome, which can be consciously acted upon in your daily life. As with all these techniques, if action is taken in response to the dream, it can result in profound changes. Changes that may not previously have been considered.

Method for using the theme to analyse your dream

Spend some time identifying the theme of the dream. It might be worth re-capping what was covered in session 2: understanding the language of dreams. Often you will be able to identify the theme by asking yourself what is the main energy of the dream. What are you, as the dream character, physically doing and who or what are you doing this with/to? A good method to use is to take away all the detail from the dream, e.g. names, things, places etc... and leave only the action. This will often leave you with an identifiable theme that you can write down in as few words as possible. Next, ask yourself how the "dreaming you" was affected by the events in the dream. Again try and write as briefly as possible. Now try and match the theme and the affect to a specific area of your life; the symbols, images and environment of the dream may provide useful clues for this, but take care not to be distracted from the main task. You should then write down any questions that the dream affect prompts you to ask of yourself or the dream character(s). Attempt now to answer those questions on a conscious level, taking care to relate the issues to events occurring in your life. Finally, decide on an outcome. What do you need to do (or think) in order to resolve the issue raised in the dream? Do you need to modify your behaviour towards, or your reaction to, the dream event? Depending on the nature of the dream you may want to adapt this method slightly. For instance; in observer dreams it may be more appropriate to describe how a certain action affected the main character rather than you as the dreamer. If you do this, you must nevertheless assume that this dream character represents yourself.

Example of TAQO analysis

The dreamer is a woman in her mid-twenties. Her boyfriend is married and no one knows about the affair, not even her closest friend.

Dream Title: I die in an aeroplane crash

I'm in an aeroplane, my boyfriend is with me, and everything is quite normal and calm. Suddenly, there's an awful engine noise and the plane starts to nose dive. Everyone's screaming and running around the plane, panic-stricken. I look round for my boyfriend. I'm terrified. The door at the rear of the plane is open and he's standing by it, putting on a life jacket. I scream to him to help me but he ignores me. I go over to him; there are no more life jackets left. I beg him to take me with him but he jumps out of the plane on his own. I'm in the plane when it crashes.

Theme: Back to earth with a crash.

Affect: I'm terrified. I'm being abandoned. I'm panic stricken. I'm going to die.

Question: Has my boyfriend given any indication that he might abandon me?

Answer: No, I believe he loves me as much as I love him. At the moment I do feel like we're "flying high" though this dream has greatly troubled me.

Action/Outcome: The dreamer assumed that the dream was just portraying her own insecurity about the affair but decided to ask her boyfriend what he thought about her dream. However, before she had chance to do so, a third party discovered the affair and the boyfriend ended the relationship immediately and quite callously. She did indeed feel abandoned and had to cope with the resultant emotional trauma on her own. Clearly her dream ego knew far more about the boyfriend's feelings towards her than her conscious self did. If this dreamer had understood and trusted her dream ego, she could have either prepared herself for what ensued, or ended the relationship herself.

A cautionary note

Dreams of death are very common and should never be interpreted as an impending, physical death. The human psyche almost always portrays the death of a part of itself as an actual physical death in one form or another. The part that dies may be a relationship that ends, a job that finishes or a stage of life being left behind, (puberty, menopause, even the birth of a child). It's as though the psyche needs to mourn the passing of things that were once important, to allow us to let go and get on with our lives.

5.5: Plot analysis (a good story)

As any professional writer will tell you, good plots have their foundation in characterisation and conflict, reflecting human emotions that are identifiable to the reader. A good story has a definite theme centred around some sort of conflict. As the story unfolds, the conflict reaches a climax, (i.e. things can't get any worse) and this results in the hero/heroine acting in such a way as to resolve the conflict. In addition to the main plot, stories often contain sub-plots peripheral to the main action, these add extra dimensions and more interest. They too will have an identifiable Theme, Conflict, Climax and (possibly) Resolution. Reviewing your dream as if it were a work of fiction is a fun thing to do and will show you that most dreams are quite adept at telling a good story. It will also help you evaluate your dream more objectively, and that can lead to deep insights.

Unlike works of fiction, however, some dreams taken alone will sometimes seem to be incomplete, especially if they don't seem to offer a resolution to the conflict. Often this is because the subconscious is dealing with a real life soap opera, which is being presented in instalments as the life situation develops and unfolds. So, in the absence of an identifiable resolution, it's likely that the subconscious has not yet finished mulling over this particular problem.

As the majority of dreams are anxiety dreams and all anxiety dreams have, at their root, some sort of conflict, you'll never be short of dreams to work on using this technique. The conflict may be internal, perhaps you are being forced to act in a way that is contrary to your nature, or it may be a conflict with another person that is adversely affecting your life in some way. Whatever the reason, this technique will be useful in discovering the cause and effect and may even lead to a resolution of the problem.

Method for plot analysis

Imagine your dream is a stage play or TV drama, which you are charged with reviewing. Begin your review by writing a synopsis about the place where the dream occurs. Add to this the identification, and description, of all the characters and any props that have been used.

Having done this, read the dream through very carefully a number of times and identify the development of the plot(s) and the associated developing tensions within the dream story. How many plots / sub-plots are there? Within each subplot identify, and make notes on, the Theme and the Conflict. Next, identify the climax that follows the appearance of each conflict – this is the culmination of the tension that has been building. Something decisive happens or changes occur. The climax may appear almost immediately or may be separated from the conflict by another sub-plot. Finally look for any resolutions or outcomes, i.e. the way in which the dreaming self has resolved the conflict. Bear in mind that resolutions do not always result in happy endings and the outcome may be something you find abhorrent or distasteful. The absence of a resolution usually indicates that the conflict has not yet been resolved in the subconscious and so you may choose to seek a solution on a conscious level.

Once you have dissected your dream in this way, you need to try and identify the area of your life to which it relates, with specific reference to the conflicts. Once you've done this you can then decide whether the dream contains an acceptable resolution to your current problem. If it does, then you can act on this in your waking life. If it doesn't, try asking yourself how you would like the story to end. What would need to happen for this story to come to a satisfactory conclusion?

Example of plot analysis

Dream title: I'm having to deal with rude people

I find a leak coming through the ceiling in my house. It's only a little drip but it gets worse and starts to pour through the ceiling. I go outside and see water gushing out of an out building. I go inside to investigate. I find a well-to-do farmer in there, discharging gallons of water onto the ground. I ask him what he's doing. He says, in a very dismissive manner, "Oh don't worry, I'm just getting rid of all this water." Reading between the lines, I know that he means, "It's my land, I can do as I please." I'm very angry and say, "Do you realise how bad mannered you are? You're a really obnoxious man!" He acknowledges what I've said and shrugs his shoulders like he doesn't care.

A short while later I'm back inside my house, in the kitchen sitting round a table with four other women. I'm telling them a story but two of the women have picked up a piece of paper and are reading it and laughing amongst themselves. They're not listening to me. I shout across the table at them, "Oh, you are so rude!"

Synopsis by the dreamer:
The story begins inside a house, moves to an outbuilding, and then back to the house. The main character is angry because people don't seem to be considering the consequence of their actions and they are not listening to her. She's a rather aggressive woman, who imagines slights where none are intended. She has three antagonists, (a well-to-do farmer and two female friends). There are two other passive females who play no part in the action. The props comprise only water and a kitchen table.

Main Plot

The Conflict: Other people are not giving the main character the respect she thinks she deserves

The Climax: She aggressively tells these people how rude and obnoxious they are

The Resolution: None given. Her reactions seem over the top and ineffectual

Subplots

Water coming through the ceiling

Conflict: dripping water may damage the ceiling

Climax: the drip changes into a torrent

Resolution: the main character goes outside to investigate

Conversation with Farmer

Conflict: a farmer, who owns the land, is discharging water without a thought for the main character, he sees nothing wrong with what he's doing

Climax: She tells him he's bad mannered and obnoxious

Resolution: he seems to accept what she says but doesn't seem to care what she thinks

Meeting with friends

Conflict: main character is telling a story to four friends and half of them aren't listening

Climax: She tells them they're very rude

Resolution: None given

The dreamer remembered that a couple of days before this dream she had been involved in an altercation with an internet shopping company. The goods she had ordered failed to arrive on the stipulated date and, after many phone calls in which she was passed from person to person, she was eventually told that the goods were out of stock. She was persuaded to purchase more expensive items that were in stock, only to have exactly the same thing happen again. Very upset and quite distressed after many days of trying to obtain a resolution, she told me that she ended up yelling down the phone at them like a screaming banshee! This didn't get her anywhere at all and only led to her feeling even more helpless and ineffectual.

The fact that the dream begins inside the home and then moves to an out building is significant. It suggests that the issue is a problem that is affecting all areas of her life; both in close relationships and also with people outside of her social circle. Note too that water in dreams always represents emotions. So a slow drip that turns into a torrent represents minor emotional stress that gets out of control.

Conscious resolution

Having dissected the dream in this way, the dreamer saw immediately the parallels to her waking life, extending beyond the altercation with the internet company. The dream highlighted aggressive, reactive behaviour. It horrified her to think that she may indeed be reacting like this whenever she felt she was being ignored or made to feel unimportant. The dream put her on alert, to watch out for this type of reaction; a reaction that she knows is totally ineffective and inappropriate when one needs other people's cooperation.

Action

To help her in her resolve, the dreamer booked herself onto an assertiveness course so that she will be better able to handle difficult situations in the future.

5.6: Change perspective

Sometimes we're too close to a dream to identify the issue it's dealing with. As we learned earlier, the ego is a powerful censor that operates to support and maintain our self-image; often dismissing or distorting information that suggests we may not be who, or what, we believe ourselves to be. On a conscious level, therefore, we may be totally unaware of some of our personality traits or behaviours and make excuses to justify actions that we would otherwise find unacceptable either in ourselves or in other people. This method involves taking your dream and imagining it is the dream of one of your dream characters. In this way, you will be able to write about yourself in the dream from another person's perspective. You may be surprised at the insights you gain into yourself by what you see. So, for instance, if I should dream of someone verbally abusing me, I will experience what it is to be the aggressor by putting myself in his or her shoes. Having done this, I will be in a better position to ask myself if I'm behaving like this in some area of my life, or indeed if my behaviour invites such a response from other people in my waking reality.

Method for changing perspective

Choose a dream to work on and identify a prominent character in the dream, this may be someone you know in reality or it may not. It does not even have to be another person; it can be anything in the dream that can be assigned an identity, such as an animal or even an inanimate object such as a vase of flowers.

Re-write the entire dream from this other character's perspective, both emotionally and spatially. Perhaps your dream begins, "I'm out walking my dog but it keeps sitting down and refusing to move..." You may re-write the dream from the dog's viewpoint by beginning, "The person who controls me is dragging me along behind them. I sit down and refuse to move because I don't want to be controlled in this way."

Example of changing perspective

Dream title: Mixed messages

I'm at work, in the general office, talking to the Head of the organisation. I'm asking her who is responsible for a particular area, as I need to ask them a question. She seems annoyed that I don't know and gives me a sharp slap across my face! It doesn't hurt but it's a bit of a shock. She immediately puts her arm around my shoulder and walks me out of the office. She's whispering in my ear, that she had to slap me because she needed to show the other employees that she's totally impartial, and in that respect it will do my credibility good because the other employees will see that I'm not being treated favourably. I have the impression that she's telling me that I'm her favourite employee but she doesn't want the others to know.

Re-written from the perspective of the Head of the organisation.

One of my employees is asking me who is responsible for a particular area within the organisation. I think she should know the answer and so I slap her across her face to punish her for not knowing. I assume that all the other employees have seen me do this. She looks shocked. I put my arm round her shoulders in a friendly manner and lead her out of the office. I whisper in her ear, so no one else can hear, that the slap was to show the other employees that she's no different to the rest of them and isn't being treated more favourably. I tell her it will give her more credibility with her peers. She seems to accept this and is quite amiable about it. How can I have any respect for someone who allows themselves to be knocked about and manipulated like that!

This technique assumes that all dream characters are aspects of the dreamer and so here the dreamer had to assume that her boss was an aspect of herself. When she had the dream, she had been in the job about six months and was finding it difficult to integrate. She reports that she was over-qualified for the position but lacked hands-on experience in the line of business. However, she had been offered the position because she had the skill and experience that was needed by the organisation in order for them to move into a new area. Unfortunately her peers were resentful of her appointment, feeling that they should have been considered for this new line of work. Management, realising they had acted outside of recommended protocols with regard to the hiring of staff, decided not to allocate the new work to the dreamer. At the time, the dreamer had no knowledge of why the work she'd been promised hadn't materialised. Instead she was expected to do exactly the same work as the rest of her peers, and was left feeling that her lack of experience undermined her credibility. The dreamer, therefore, was feeling isolated and inadequate because of the back-room machinations and office politics; none of which she was privy to.

When asked what she thought the dream meant, she had initially concluded that it was simply telling her about the mixed messages being given to her by her employer. On the one hand she was being told that her skills were invaluable to the organisation, but yet her skills were not being utilised. When she re-wrote the dream she recognised immediately that she was beating herself up about her lack of expertise in the line of work she was now doing. She also suggested that the dream seems to highlight the strategy she had been employing of voluntarily exhibiting her inadequacies in front of her peers; a strategy that she hoped would gain their empathy and friendship. She said how the dream painfully highlights the way in which she is compromising her dignity and academic integrity in an effort to be accepted, and in the process was losing her self-respect. In other words, she was so desperately trying to fit in to the organisation that she was oblivious to the damage she was doing to herself.

Action:

After analysing the dream in this way, the dreamer concluded that she was in an untenable position, a round peg in a square hole, and started making plans to leave this organisation.

5.7: Amplification

This technique does not really stand alone but is usually used in conjunction with one or more of the other techniques covered. As you begin to work with your dreams, you'll discover that some dreams contain ideas, symbols or characters that are difficult to relate to your everyday life. Often these represent archetypes or archetypal situations that are playing out in real life. An archetype is a simple, idealised example of a person or situation that human beings, throughout time, have understood and modelled themselves on, often unconsciously. Common archetypes are such things as The Hero, The Trickster, The Wise Old Man, The Nurturing Mother, The Magician or The Child. Common archetypal situations include death and rebirth, idealised romantic love, transformation of animals into people, sacrifice of self or others. Tarot cards are based on archetypes, as are most of our well-loved fairy tales.

It was Carl Jung who brought the idea of archetypes into mainstream psychology. He believed that they resided within, what he termed, the collective unconscious. This is a reservoir of human knowledge and experience accessible to all, regardless of life experience or culture. He described it as a collective human memory store and he used Amplification to explore the archetypes contained therein. Through his research into mythology, he proposed that the psychological changes that occur as a person matures and then declines, prompts a series of inner directives that issue from the self (Dream Ego) rather than from the conscious ego. He proposed that from birth to midlife, we are involved primarily with biological and social functioning and that the period from middle age to death is concerned more with cultural and spiritual matters. He highlighted the fact that the transition from one stage of life to the next seems to be a time of potential crisis.

Indeed, rites of passage have evolved in many societies in order to help the individual make the transitions as smoothly as possible. Each transition may be archetypically represented by the death of the previous stage of life and a rebirth into the new. In modern day Western society, where the hard sciences reign supreme and religious activity is declining, there is no such help available to the majority of people. The midlife crisis has become a familiar term in our modern world with many men and women finding themselves involved in various kinds of upheaval during this stage. The upheaval may take the form of divorce, relocation to a new area or a complete change of occupation. These upheavals are often symptomatic of the attempt to make (or avoid) the transition to the next stage. For others, it's a vague feeling that there is no excitement or zest in life anymore, that the magic of life has gone. This often leads to depression and a deep feeling of dissatisfaction with one's life. It may be the start of a highly critical period, if not self-criticism then criticism of the life partner, or the work environment or neighbourhood. Some people turn to alcohol or promiscuity to avoid confrontation with the deeper issues within themselves. Others manage to sail through this transition without even acknowledging that anything is changing, plodding on through the same daily routines or spending vast sums of money in an effort to remain physically youthful.

No matter how we try, on a conscious level, to avoid these transitions, the psyche must accept them and adapt itself accordingly. It's at times like this when archetypal imagery may appear in our dreams. Examination of the dream imagery can lead to a deeper understanding of oneself and, ultimately, to an acceptance of the natural progression of life.

In addition to having to cope with the transitional changes of life, Jung believed that man has a soul that is constantly striving to re-unite the different aspects of self that have become fragmented. He called this process individuation and believed the process was complete when the conscious and unconscious elements become united in a sort of mystical marriage. In his view, very few people ever attain this union and the majority of human beings barely get beyond the starting post. So, whilst he saw the whole process of life in terms of an inner, probably genetically determined, blueprint of birth, reproduction and death, he was also convinced that the ultimate goal of the entire process was self-realisation through individuation.

The reason for this, he believed, is;

> *".... so that the creator may become conscious of His creation, and man conscious of himself."*

Jung believed that the archetypal imagery the subconscious uses, cannot be adequately explained by the personal consciousness. He devised the technique of Amplification to elucidate the dream image by reference to mythology and cultural heritage. This, he believed, would illustrate our current stage of life's journey and help us to let go of the past and accept the new and help us integrate all the fragmented parts of our being. He believed that when our psyche is grappling with such important issues we tend to experience what he termed big dreams. These are the dreams that are rarely forgotten, the epics; the dreams we cannot understand and yet sense their importance on a deeper level.

Amplification was, he believed, a way of seeing the bigger picture. It's a chance to transcend the petty problems of our everyday life and deal with the transitional changes that are occurring.

Method for amplification

Jung's "big dreams" don't occur very often for most people. They are often recognisable because they include archetypal characters or situations. For instance; you may dream of a hero or heroine figure; a Magician or a wise old man. Such images are archetypal and are not just characters that represent themselves; they encompass a whole mythology. Fairy tales use archetypal characters, this is probably why they are well loved, generation after generation; because they appeal to our subconscious. If you don't have one of these dreams to draw on, choose a dream that contains an image or symbol that you feel is somewhat alien to your waking consciousness; an image that seems to have appeared out of nowhere and doesn't appear to be part of the day's residue.

Explore the meaning of the chosen image(s) by firstly writing down any personal associations you have. Don't build on the associations you make but return to the image or symbol each time. Next, add associations that are determined by your culture. For instance; the image of a man living rough in a forest, living off the land, may prompt personal associations of the tree dwellers who have tried to save our woodland from developers. Maybe you have a secret wish to live like that, or maybe you know someone who does. Cultural associations may be to do with a Hermit or a Woodcutter, someone choosing to live that way in order to commune with nature.

Now, expand your knowledge of the image by exploring the stories, myths and legends associated with the image, this can be done by researching in books or on the internet, or any other means at your disposal. Check out folklore anthologies and archetypal meanings. Once all the information is gathered, try and ascertain the meaning of the dream in the context of the phase of your life you are currently experiencing. Remember that archetypal situations are not particularly concerned with our everyday pressing reality. It's important that you look beyond your everyday transient problems, and address the bigger issues in your life. For instance; your children may have grown and flown the nest. On a conscious level you may be enjoying the peace and quiet but psychically you may be experiencing a loss. Whatever your feelings, on a deeper level you will be adapting to a life situation that is highlighting the passage of time and the initiation into another phase of your life; a phase where youth and the pressing needs of rearing children play no part. This major life change, rather than the outer event that has caused it, may well be the subject of many of your dreams. Archetypal dreams are not concerned with the loss, but with the transition from parenthood to old age and the way in which you will need to adapt to that changing self-image.

If you've been recording your dreams for a while, look back and see if you've dreamed of the image before. If so, interpret the dreams collectively, paying attention to the dates and the progression of events in your life at that time; pay particular attention to how you were feeling at the time of the dream(s).

Example of using amplification

Dream title: The old crone burns the scrubland to get rid of the mischief maker

I'm walking through a bleak, scrub type landscape when I see an old woman setting fire to bushes and undergrowth. I feel she's doing wrong and isn't a good person. I also see someone who seems to be inherently evil; up to mischief, though I'm not sure what he's doing. As I watch the old woman, I suddenly realise that she's setting fire to the vegetation to get rid of the power of this mischief maker and to keep it away from the area. I manage to take control of the mischief maker and stop him doing any more mischief.

Later I decide to replay a recording of everything that had happened so I can have a better understanding of what had gone on. I review all the things that had at first appeared to be bad but now see that they are part of the good of the place. I check the work of the old woman and now see her as the archetypal old crone; a sort of grandmother whose actions and lessons are not always very palatable but they work towards the greater good nonetheless. I check the countryside to make sure everything is as it should be. But as I play it all back, the mischief maker tries to break away from me. I call him back and tell him to stay and do as he's told. I feel I have a lot of personal power and don't doubt my ability to control him.

The dreamer is a woman going through the menopause. She reported that, around the time of the dream, she was feeling that she had given away all her personal power and had become immobile and ineffective. She recognised the mischief maker as the chattering monkey part of herself that constantly reminds her of past hurt and those things she wanted to keep hold of but had to give up; causing her to live with the limiting beliefs she now had about herself. On a superficial level, she saw this dream as a portrayal of herself as a woman on her way to old age, trying to control the internal dialogue that was dragging her into depression.

Amplification of the dream

Volumes have been written about the concept of the archetypal Crone, much of which has comforted and empowered women in this stage of life. Here I give only a flavour of what an amplification of the image uncovered. Mythology teaches us about the triple form of the Goddess; Virgin, Mother and Crone, and how all three exist in the human psyche. On a personal level, a woman moves through all three personifications throughout her life. The most difficult transition to make is the transition to Crone. At the menopause, women stand at the boundary between past experiences, youth left behind, and an uncertain future of becoming old and losing sexual attractiveness and vibrancy. Often women at this stage of life describe themselves as having become invisible.

When a culture has no word, nor inclination, to acknowledge the existence of 'wise elder women', society sees this ancient aspect of the feminine only in her negative forms. She's the one who brings death to our old way of being, to our lives as we have known them, and to our embodied selves. Over time, and in recent history, the Crone became associated with the dark side of the feminine; the withered old hag, the witch. This is a shame because she is a part of the natural rhythm of birth, death and rebirth and is perhaps the most powerful of all the archetypes.

"Wise women," in the past, were honoured because they had the power of life and death. They symbolised maturity and authority; they were attuned to nature and to instinct. They incorporated both dark and light, life and death, creation and destruction, form and dissolution. They were women over whom men had no sexual control. This is as true for women at this stage of their life today, as it always was. All you need do is recognise it. Accept the power that this archetype confers and embrace the Crone in all her wisdom and all her glory.

The Crone was healer, seer and medicine woman and when death arrived with inexorable certainty, she was the mid-wife for the transition to another life. (Hall 1992)

Conclusion

This dream is most certainly what Carl Jung would have described as a big dream with big medicine. It depicts the Crone almost exactly as she is depicted in mythology and is a wonderful example of an archetype plucked straight from Jung's collective unconscious. The dreamer at first thinks that the old woman is evil; she's destroying the land. But then she realises that her only intention is to banish the mischief maker. The dreamer, as an impartial observer, begins to understand that the Crone is there to heal the land, to burn what is dead, and thus clear the ground for new growth.

Action

Following the amplification, the dreamer was able to view her present life situation as a time for growth rather than decay; growth into a new way of life. She acknowledged the achievements that had provided a solid foundation on which to build her future security. In re-claiming her personal power, she found the strength within her to face up to her fears about growing old, and she began to work hard at loving her wrinkles instead of hating them. The dream had provided a powerful tool for visualisation, and she used it whenever she felt despondent. Seeing the old woman setting fire to the scrubland, to banish the mischief maker and assist nature in her efforts to re-populate the area with lush vegetation, empowered and re-assured her. Rather than retiring into the shadows of her former life, as she had been doing, she resolved to play centre stage. The energy of fire enabled her to live with more enthusiasm and confidence than she'd ever done when she was younger.

Session 6:
Start to Change
your Life

"Dreams are like stars... You may never touch them, but if you follow them they will lead you to your destiny."

Session 6: Start to Change your Life

6.1: What is it you want?

"So tell me what you want, what you really, really want?"
Spice Girls

Spend a few minutes turning this question over in your mind. What do you want out of life? If your Fairy Godmother suddenly appeared before you and said you could have anything you wanted, what would you choose?

Be reasonable; let's face it, having a torrid love affair with George Cluney is never going to happen! Whilst I don't want to put limits on your hopes and dreams, I want you to choose something that seems reasonable to achieve, but is currently out of reach. The reason for this is that I don't want you to fall at the first hurdle and give up trying. The big things, those things that seem impossible, can come later, when you've completed this course.

Of course, deciding what we really, really want is so easy to say and so difficult to do. I'm sure we all know someone from our school days who always knew what they wanted to be when they grew up and remained focussed on that goal. Those people are usually very successful in their chosen careers. Those of us who could never really decide exactly what it was that turned us on, ended up either flitting from job to job, career to career, marriage to marriage, or ended up in a job, or relationship, that was convenient and safe. How was it for you? But whether you feel you've achieved nothing, or feel you've achieved a lot, there's always something else to aim for; whether it be peace of mind, service to others or more material security. In the end, we're all searching for something. If you don't know what that something is, chances are, you'll never find it, and even if you do, you won't know you found it until you've lost it again.

Exercise 8: Using Dream Incubation to identify what you want

Take at least thirty minutes to write a list of all the things you think you might like to have or achieve.

I'm hoping you've got a long list of things that you'd like to achieve in your future. What I want you to do now, is arrange them in groups of why you want them. Some of the things may sit in more than one group, that's fine, put them in as many groups as seems appropriate. When you're looking for the whys, try and reduce each wish to one fundamental desire, something that's the "bottom line", something that can't be reduced to anything else. For instance; if asked why you've always wanted to visit Egypt, you might say it's because you've always had a fascination for the Pyramids. Why? Maybe, you enjoy history and would like to see these places. Why? You're curious. Why? Because you thirst for some adventure, escape, freedom. The underlying driver could be any of these things, or something else entirely. Just try and make sure that you reach that place where the buck stops.

Example of achievements

Personal achievement	Emotional Security	Financial security	Adventure
Write a book Run a marathon Learn to play piano	Get married Mend a relationship	Get a pay rise Change career Win the lottery	Run a marathon Change career Visit Egypt

I've used four groups in my example, but you will use as many groups as you need.

Meditate on your list over the next few days. Pin the list up where you'll see it constantly; on your fridge, near your desk, over your bed are just some of the places you could consider. Ask yourself, would you be following your heart if you pursued these things? Remember what we said in the introduction. A path with no heart is not a path you should be going along. If you want to add things to your list, or take things away, as the days go by, do so. When you feel you've got a complete list, go back to the work you did for Session 4 (Becoming more aware). How does what you discovered about yourself there, fit in with your hopes and wishes for the future? Are there any contradictions? For instance, if you think you crave adventure but have a deep-seated need to feel secure, you'll probably not go on the back-packing trip you're dreaming of until you've resolved that particular conflict.

So, having regard to what you've already discovered about yourself, choose just one thing from your list; the one thing that you feel will be most beneficial to you at this time but that gives you that excited, fluttering feeling in the pit of your stomach when you think about it. If you don't get this feeling with anything you've listed, then you need to find something that does stir your passion and enthusiasm before going any further. Make a note of what you've chosen below:

> **The achievement I'm going to work on is:**
>
> ....
>
> ....

Now, ask your subconscious how you can go about achieving this. What must you do, what steps should you take, how do you begin? Use the Incubation method already covered in Exercise 6, but this time record all your dreams over a period of a week, each night making the same affirmation, carefully tailored to get the answer you desire. You could write your choice down and put it under your pillow. You should end up with at least five dreams. If you've become proficient at recall, you could end up with an awful lot more!

Here are some suggestions to illustrate what form your affirmations might take. Bear in mind that affirmations you construct yourself will be far more powerful.

"What's the first step I must take to realise my dream of . . . . "

"Where will I find the resources?"

"Who, what, when will help me achieve this dream?"

"How will I feel when I've achieved this?"

In the next section we will look at ways in which you can work with your resulting series of dreams in order to understand their wisdom and take appropriate action.

6.2: Working with a dream series

In this section, instead of looking at just one dream in isolation, we're going to look at the series of dreams from your last incubation (Exercise 8). It's thought that dreams occurring during the same sleep period, or over a few nights, often explore variations on the same theme, even without an incubation. However, this is often not very apparent from a cursory examination of the dream material, due to the fact that the subconscious will latch onto any convenient symbol to illustrate whatever it is reviewing. Your dreaming mind explores issues from many different angles; rehearsing all possible outcomes. So, although the issue under consideration remains the same, the stories that unfold can be dramatically different. But if you look closely enough, you'll realise that there are always subtle connections, often difficult to recognise on a conscious level. In view of this, don't be surprised if, on the surface, your incubated dreams appear to bear no relation to each other.

Also be aware that your dreams may be telling you that what you most desire would not be good for you. If this happens, you need to find the courage to abandon that particular goal and look for the reason your dreams are putting the dampers on it. There will always be a good reason. Remember, dreams arise from the core self; the intuitive part of you that is only concerned with your health and well-being; the part of you that wants to walk the path of the heart. When the wishes of the conscious ego are at odds with this, you can be sure that your dreams will let you know. Of course, you can ignore this advice and carry on regardless. If you do this, the chances are you'll look back with hindsight, at some point in the future, and realise that your dream warnings were well founded.

A note on recurring dreams

Recurring dreams are those dreams that are dealing with long standing issues and so they often occur over extended periods of time. Often though, because the subconscious is working through the issue, it's only the theme that recurs rather than the actual dream content and so they are not always easy to spot. For instance; if I'm having trouble emotionally withdrawing from a past relationship, I may have dreams about bags, suitcases or holdalls. Perhaps my dreaming self will try to pack too many things into a small suitcase, another time it might be struggling to carry too many bags, and yet another dream might find me discovering a bag I didn't know I had with me. The environment of all the dreams may be completely different but the theme is the same; i.e. too much (emotional) baggage. The methods I'm going to present here work just as well on recurring dreams as they do on a dream series from a short time frame. But, please note, that if you're suffering from recurring dreams that are the result of post-traumatic stress, I strongly recommend that you seek professional help.

In exercise 8 (using dream incubation to identify what you want) you incubated a series of dreams to try and identify how you can achieve whatever it is you've decided you really want. Hopefully, you will have at least two dreams to work on, possibly many more.

Now it's time to work with those dreams and identify what action you can take to achieve your goal. I expect this exercise will take you at least a few days, maybe longer. You'll need to do a lot of lateral thinking, so make sure your grey matter is ready and willing to be flexed. Although working on a dream series is far more time consuming than working on single dreams, it gives a great deal more insight into how your mind works. It also provides an astonishing illustration of the wonderfully creative way in which your subconscious supports you in your quest for wholeness. So let this process take, however long it takes; don't rush it.

> **Exercise 9: Analysing more than one dream at the same time**
>
> Synopsis of the method
>
> Step 1 Write down each dream and allocate a number
>
> Step 2 Give each dream a title
>
> Step 3 Analyse each dream individually
>
> Step 4 Taking all dreams together, which elements are similar and which are contradictory?
>
> Step 5 Write a brief synopsis of each dream
>
> Step 6 Translate each dream into a short, personal statement. Note down the most important point.
>
> Step 7 Merge the dreams into one story
>
> Step 8 What action(s) is (are) suggested by the dreams?
>
> More details about each step are on the following pages.

Step 1: Begin by writing out each dream on a separate piece of paper, using the first person, present tense. For example: "I'm in a restaurant," rather than, "I was in a restaurant." Include the date of the dream and, if possible, the time. Number them in the order they were dreamed. Some dream researchers believe that dreams experienced at the beginning of the night relate to past experiences, brought into a dream to help us understand a current situation. Dreams in the middle of the night will incorporate images and experiences from the last couple of days and dreams just before waking contain the resolution or solution to the issue that initiated the first dream. This theory is based on the assumption that dreaming is a way of examining daily experiences to help us maintain and update our internal, emotional picture of ourselves and they do this by mixing old memory images with more recent ones.

Step 2: Give each dream a title that gives a flavour of the theme of the dream, in as few words as possible.

Step 3: Go back to "session 5: Working with your dreams", and, using all or some of the techniques described, attempt an analysis of all the dreams individually. If you have an unmanageable number, I suggest you limit yourself to six dreams initially, perhaps just taking the dreams recorded on the first and second nights of the incubation. Make a note of your interpretation on the same sheet of paper as the dream itself. Bear in mind that this interpretation is not set in stone; you may find you need to modify it as you progress through this method and uncover more information.

Step 4: Explore Commonalities: Make a list of the symbols and characters in each of the dreams. The table in the step 4 of the worked example that follows illustrates how to do this. Note any commonalities. Where a symbol or character appears in more than one of the dreams write this down in the centre of a new sheet of paper. Around this word place all the dream connections, making sure you include the number of the dream. Work outwards from these, adding all the thoughts, descriptions or associations you have with that unique symbol, like spokes radiating from a wheel hub. For example, if all the dreams have an element of escape or running away, you may find that what you are running away from is different in each dream. In this case, the centre of your hub may be, "Running Away", with the first layer of the spokes being, "Dream 1 Tiger, Dream 2 Monster, Dream 3 Husband."

The next layer would be your personal associations to each of these symbols. See figure 3 for an example of the form this diagram should take. Once completed, this diagram can be used to gain an in depth understanding of the elements within the dreams and the role they are currently playing in your life. If commonalities are not immediately apparent, look for elements that could link the dreams together. For instance; you may have a garden gnome in one dream and a flower bed in another – the common element here would be a garden or gardening and it is this that you would put into the centre of your diagram, with the gnome and the flower bed making the first layer of the spokes. It can also be very useful to use this method to explore all the helpful characters in the dreams to see what attributes and strengths they/you possess that can be used to help you achieve your goal. You'll find an illustration of this in the example that follows. Do the same for any unhelpful characters, being aware that these are aspects of yourself that are hindering your progress.

Step 5: Synopsis: Write a brief synopsis of each dream, (the dream, not the interpretation).

Step 6: Translation and most salient point: Next, draw up a three column table, (as shown in the example later in the book). In the first column, write the number assigned to the dream. Go through each synopsis and even more briefly translate it into a personal statement about yourself. For example; your synopsis might read, "I was in a Church at the funeral of a close friend. The Church was full and people were trying to stop the Priest from conducting the ceremony. It was very upsetting." Your translation may be something like; "A part of me, that I wanted to keep hold of, has died." Write this translation in the second column. It's important that you assume that all symbols, images and actions are aspects of yourself, in other words assume that your friend/sister/ husband/wife/stranger is in the dream because of a character trait that you either have or that you need. Try and keep your notes as brief as possible, this will aid clarity and make the task more manageable. You can always go back and add more detail later.

Once you've done this, pick out the most salient emotion or action in each translation and enter this into the third column. Try and limit yourself to one word if you can. For example, in the illustration used above, the word that sums up the most salient point might be Death.

Look for a progression or advancement of ideas that indicates that your subconscious is working out how you can achieve your goal. If the dreams remain essentially the same, without seeming to present any ideas for action, it could be an indication that there's a blockage somewhere and you may need to identify and deal with this before you can get a result.

Now write a conclusion; a statement that you can easily remember, that embodies the overall message of the dream series.

Step 7: Merge the dreams: This step requires you to be very creative and have some fun with your dreams. I want you to merge all the dreams into one but in such a way that they tell an empowering story. You can do this sequentially or you can overlay them. The nature of the dreams will dictate the best way to approach this. It isn't necessary to use all the detail from every dream and you can add tidbits of wisdom and insight that you've discovered along the way. You may find you have to write a few drafts before you get a coherent merged dream. Imagine you're writing a synopsis of a block buster movie, with you as the hero/heroine.

Your merged dream will serve to empower you whenever you feel yourself slipping away from your goal or faltering in your resolution to make changes in your life. Pin it up on your bathroom wall, put it on your bedside table or keep it on your person. As the days or weeks pass by, add to it, change it, do whatever you like to it, this is a message from your inner Guru. Honour it.

Step 8: Action

Make a list of all possible actions suggested by the dreams, no matter how bizarre some may seem at the moment. If you've exercised lateral thinking, you should by now have a wealth of ideas about what you can do to make your wish a reality, or at least progress towards it. In the next session you will use this list to write an action plan for yourself.

And by way of a footnote; watch out for further dreams that seem to deal with the same issue. Are the dreams changing? If so, do they suggest a different course of action?

Example of how to work with a dream series

Because this is a lengthy process, and space is limited, the following example uses only four dreams, but you can use this technique on however many dreams you've selected to work with. The dreams that follow are taken from my own journal at a time when I was struggling to decide whether or not to take early retirement, on a very small work's pension, from a secure, well-paid job. I'd never been happy in the job and so this was a well-timed opportunity for me to leave. I was still eight years away from state retirement age and so, in theory, would still be a viable contender in the job market. The decision should have been very easy to make but it wasn't, and I found myself immobilised by my indecision. The deadline for applying was fast approaching and, if I didn't act soon, the opportunity would be lost and may never come again. On a conscious level I was procrastinating about the loss of financial security, even though I felt I could manage on a low income if I had to; I'd done it before and I could do it again. I knew that if I took this opportunity I would have more time to pursue my writing, a prospect that filled me with joy and excitement. Even as a child, I had ambition to be a writer and so this would be the fulfilment of a lifelong wish. The thought of remaining in the job, filled me with dread. Given that I had such strong reactions to both scenarios, and yet still couldn't decide, told me there was something else here of which I was not consciously aware. The question I decided to put to my dreaming mind was,

"Why am I hesitating in the pursuit of my heart's desire?"

Steps 1 to 3

Dream 1 (4 days before the decision deadline)

Dream Title: The old things are still there

I'm talking over the possibility of early retirement with Mum and my sister. I'm explaining that if I don't take it, I'll have to wait eight years to get my work's pension. Mum says, "You could be dead by then!"

Now I'm in the alley way that runs down the side of my childhood home. I say to my sister, "Look at the stone cobbles, and the cap stones on top of the wall, and the stone flags on the pavement, they're all exactly the same as they were when we were children."

We're now in the hall of the house. I'm looking at the old, peeling paint work on the stair banister. I pick at it, peeling away all the layers, and say. "Look, you can see how Dad kept painting it all those years ago." Suddenly, we decide we'd better make a quick exit before anyone discovers us as this isn't our house any more.

Initial interpretation

The dream starts with a reminder that time is running out, not just for the decision I have to make, but also for my life! This comment immediately stirs childhood memories. I see that the stones haven't changed. Stones are enduring and resilient, they don't seem to change much over a human lifetime. But stones are also hard and unfeeling. A "heart of stone" shows no emotion. A heart of stone refuses to acknowledge emotions. Are the stones representing a part of me that is stuck in the past, a part that refuses to accept that time has passed and things have changed? Or are they something from my childhood that has endured; something that I could still build on or build something from?

Inside the house, the painting, done by my Dad, has deteriorated with age and is showing the effects of the passage of time. In reality, Dad died three years before the dream. Whilst I was growing up, and especially during my teenage years, this was a stormy relationship that contributed to my low self esteem. The picking at the paint and peeling away all the layers is undoubtedly to do with the exploration of this. Houses almost always represent "self" in its entirety; the physical body and the psyche. The dream shows me what is underneath the veneer, untouched by the passage of time, and what is left (the wooden banister) is still able to help me climb the stairs. Indeed, my happiest memory of my Dad was one night when he gave me a fireman's lift up the stairs to bed. This dream is an excellent example of how the dreaming mind explores multiple issues, on multiple levels, all at the same time. The dream shows how issues from my childhood, which on a conscious level may seem to have little to do with my current problem, are affecting me in the present. This isn't the time to delve into these issues here, but note how my Dream Ego becomes aware that the owner of the house, (my conscious ego), wouldn't want me in this place, looking at the deterioration that's occurred in the paint work/veneer over the years and prying into memories that might be painful. We must leave before we're discovered.

Dream 2 (3 days before the decision deadline)

Dream Title: A lady clears all my clutter

I'm standing in a very large kitchen in what is, in the dream, my house. I seem to be limping; I think I've had a hip replacement. The kitchen is in a terrible mess – as if I'm re-decorating and in the midst of a huge upheaval. It's night time and there's a knock at the door. It's a lady. She tells me she's just calling to check that I'm alright and also checking the date of an appointment I'm supposed to have made for something. She only stays a couple of minutes. After she's gone I'm amazed that my kitchen has miraculously become tidy; I now see that the floor is covered in a blue carpet and there's a lovely rustic oak table and chairs. But then I become a bit suspicious. I wonder if she had her own reasons for calling. Had she called to see what it was like to have a limp after a hip replacement, so that she could feign it?

Initial interpretation

My mind is so full of clutter that I can't think straight. My clutter has disabled me (hip replacement which has left me with a limp). It's also stopping me from getting the nourishment I need; the kitchen is too cluttered to make a meal. My higher self, the archetypal wise mother, (who we met in the first dream), can eliminate the clutter immediately, perhaps by waving a magic wand, but a part of me is suspicious of her motives, which I suspect might be self-serving. I recall that my Mum has had both her hips replaced in reality. I'm also wondering what appointment the lady is checking up on; the association that immediately came into my mind, was the appointment we all have with the Grim Reaper!

Dream 3 (2 days before the decision deadline Time 2.30am)

Dream Title: Casting director has his eye on me

I'm at a gathering of amateur dramatists. I seem to be very popular though I'm keeping a low profile and staying on the sidelines. A girl of African descent has come over to chat to me. She's got her face very close to mine, invading my personal space, but in a very friendly manner. I can feel her breath on my cheek as she chats. Her face is covered in writing. She points out a man who is sitting in the shadows, watching what's going on. She tells me he's a professional casting director and is looking at me.

Initial interpretation

I'm involved in an amateur dramatic group in reality. It's about acting, role playing, helping back stage. Acting reminds me of Carl Jung's concept of our many different personas; the masks we present to the world. Here again there's a helpful female. Because of her close proximity, it's clear she's intent on getting her point across to me. The only association I can make to African descent is that modern humans supposedly arose out of Africa, so this could be another reference to something from the past that, like the stones, endures. With the writing all over her face, she so beautifully and eloquently draws my attention to my writing ambitions, and tells me that there may be an opportunity for me to be cast in that role.

135

Dream 4 (2 days before the decision deadline Time 6.30am)

Dream Title: I've seen the light but there's resistance

I'm in a large University lecture theatre; sitting on a curved balcony looking down on the stage. There's someone with me. The presentation is about something secret. Suddenly, bright lights are projected onto the screen at the front. I'm amazed/shocked and exclaim to my companion, "Look, look the lights!" The lights are very important and reveal that they have a grand plan that they're trying to keep from the public. The lights remind me of the lights in the film 'Close Encounters of the Third Kind.' We rush outside. There's an organisation we must tell; a sort of resistance movement. We run across the campus. A tall, dark-haired, Jewish looking man signals to us to follow him. He takes us to an underground hideout. Once inside we start to tell him that we have discovered the grand plan that is being kept secret but then others call and we have to stop talking – this isn't for their ears. They talk and talk and time is running out. The Jewish-looking man makes time speed up – oh my goodness, it's 6.15pm, the chattering people realise they must go. Now we can resume our discussion. I know that he will make a fair, considered decision.

Initial interpretation

Although the job I'm thinking of leaving is with a University, it's not the University in the dream. So, as well as indicating the dream is about the decision I must make, it also suggests that there is a lesson here, after all a University is a place of learning. Dream 2 showed that I needed clarity of thought. This dream suggests that I now have it; in a, "oh my goodness, how amazing," sort of way. My associations to the film mentioned are to do with perseverance and determination to uncover the truth. The characters, Jillian and Roy, endure physical and mental torment. They are deceived by the authorities and ridiculed by the press. Despite this, they would not be dissuaded and remained true to their goal. Eventually they were rewarded with knowing the truth; their single mindedness paid off. Jillian gets her little boy back and Roy embarks on a journey to an alien world. Also, many airmen from WW2, for whom time had stood still, were returned to a new world. The concept of contact with aliens is very apt when you consider that early retirement is a major life transition that is completely alien to someone who's worked all their life. No wonder my amazement in the dream was equal to the amazement displayed by the characters in the film. It's also interesting to note that this film was released in the year that I made a major career move; leaving a secure, well-paid career in Accountancy and Taxation to re-train as an Haute Courtier dress maker. Thus the dream seems to be allaying my fears about making the transition, on many levels. It suggests that the future holds the promise of new adventures. However, what about the Jewish resistance? I've met similar characters to this in my dreams before. He represents a shadow part of my psyche; a part that was born when I was a child, a part that arose to protect me from outside influences over which I had no control. An underground hideout is a safe place in the subconscious, a place where painful emotions can be buried away and forgotten about. The dream seems to suggest that this man would not be in favour of what the University is doing. Perhaps he's trying to safeguard my financial security. Unfortunately, the conversation that ensued was not remembered, perhaps not even dreamed, but the indication is that I needed to talk to him to explain that what was going on was not life-threatening. On the contrary, it was very exciting. It's also worth mentioning that there are dream workers who believe numbers in dreams are of great importance and should be taken as an indication of time scale. It's not necessarily an idea I subscribe to. However, numbers are always there for a reason and this should be born in mind in the analysis.

Step 4: Explore Commonalities

The main images in the dreams

Dream 1	Dream 2	Dream 3	Dream 4
Mum (advice)	Adult home	Theatre	Lecture theatre
Sister (confidant)	Kitchen	African girl (actress)	Presentation
Childhood home	Lady (helper)	Face of writing	Lights
Alley way	Clutter	Casting Director	A grand plan
Hall	Disabled		Resistance mvt
Stones			Underground
Peeling paint			Noisy people

As you'll see from the table, there don't appear to be many common images across the four dreams. This doesn't mean the dreams are not related, it simply indicates that the issue under consideration is being processed rapidly. This often happens with incubated dreams; the subconscious seems to realise that you're primed to listen and so it has no need for repetition. The notes that follow are my observations about the commonalities that are present.

➤ The most striking commonality is found in the first three dreams where, in each, there is a helpful female character; all aspects of the archetypal wise woman. It's interesting that my own Mum has had hip replacements and yet, in Dream 2, it was me that had had this operation. Perhaps this is an indication that I possess some of the "wise woman" characteristics that I happily confer on other women, specifically my Mum. This may explain the feeling in the dream that the lady was checking out my limp so she could feign the same disability. Of course, this also suggests that I have quite negative feelings connected with ageing, and suggests that one of my worries about accepting early retirement is a feeling that somehow I'll be crossing the line that separates youthfulness from old age. This fear is also alluded to in Dream 1 by Mum suggesting that I may not be here much longer, and also, of course, the deteriorating paint work and the reminder about my dead father. Apart from these archetypal wise women, there's an additional helpful character in Dream 4 in the guise of the Jewish man. The fact that I may not need the sort of help he's offering, in no way negates his role as a helper. All of these characters represent parts of my psyche that can aid my progress and development, so it's important that I understand as much about them as I can. If I do this, I'll be able to make full, conscious use of the wisdom they hold. My exploration of this is shown in Figure 3.

➤ Whilst looking at the helpful characters in these four dreams, I was struck by the absence of unhelpful characters. This is an interesting observation and one I advise you to apply to your own dreams; it could be a good way to ascertain whether the goal you are pursuing is in your best interests. The unhelpful characters that hinder us in our dreams can represent those obstacles that our subconscious places in our path to try and prevent us from compromising our well-being. They may also be aspects of our inner saboteur or shadow, in which case they will need to be healed and integrated before any real progress can be made.

➤ The house owner in dream 1, the person whom my sister and I are frightened will discover us, is my conscious ego. This is the part of me that doesn't want my dream ego rooting about, examining the deterioration. In dream 4, this aspect of myself makes another appearance in the form of the chattering "others" who talk and talk and waste precious time. It's very clear from these dreams that my conscious ego doesn't want to face up to getting old, doesn't want me crossing that threshold into old age, and it's looking likely that this is the main reason for my indecision.

➤ The first two dreams occur within a house, my childhood home. This is my personal space, my "self", me in my entirety. In addition, dreams set within a childhood home are tapping into issues, emotions or beliefs that we held during childhood. The next two dreams are in public places; a theatre where plays are performed, and a lecture theatre in a university. In my ordinary waking reality, I'm used to performing in both and so these dreams are about my public personas. Though I note that in neither of these dreams am I performing; I'm watching, waiting, learning.

➤ Time – Dream 1 looks at how time changes some things but not others. It tells me that my time may be running out. Although this is a direct reference to dying, be aware that dreams often address multiple ideas at the same time, and so this is probably also reminding me that the deadline for applying for early retirement is almost upon me. In Dream 2 we see the clutter disappear in no time at all; one minute it's there, the next minute it's gone. Dream 4 returns to the idea that time is running out and seems to be another reminder of the application deadline.

Figure 3: Expansion and Associations of the helpful Dream Characters.

A powerful reminder that these are all aspects of my inner self.

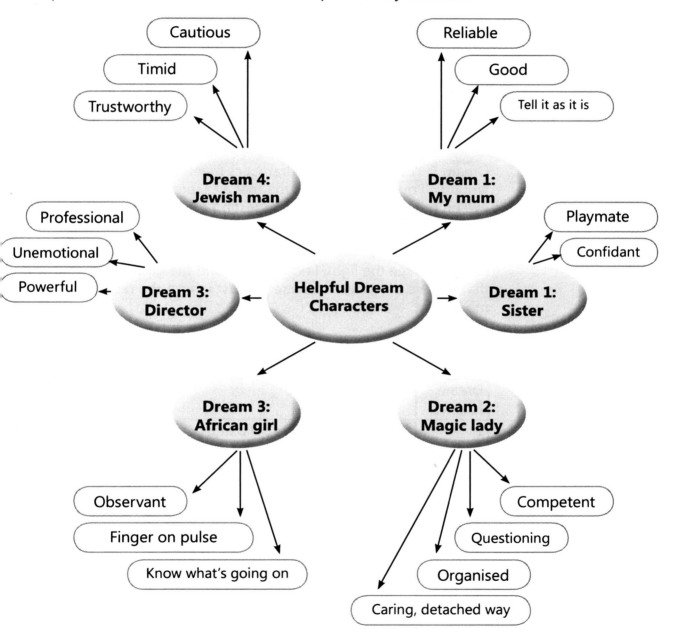

Step 5: Synopses

Dream 1: I might die before I reach normal retirement age. I look back at the past, the time when I was a child. I see how the stones, that were part of my childhood, are solid and enduring, unchanged. Inside the house, even though there is evidence of superficial deterioration, the solid foundation is still there.

Dream 2: I've had a hip replacement and am limping. I can't get proper nourishment because my kitchen is so full of clutter. A lady calls and magically makes all my clutter disappear. I wonder if she has an ulterior motive. Perhaps she wants to feign my disability?

Dream 3: I'm at an amateur dramatics meeting. A girl with writing all over her face tells me that a casting director has his eye on me. She seems to be suggesting that I may be offered a professional role.

Dream 4: I'm watching a presentation at a University when I suddenly see the light. I now understand the grand plan that they've tried to keep secret. I must inform the resistance movement.

Step 6:

The main points within the dreams

Dream No.	Translation	Most salient point
1	My foundations are solid and enduring, whilst my body is deteriorating.	Time passing
2	My mind is cluttered with many thoughts. I need clarity.	Clutter
3	Becoming a professional writer is a possibility.	Hope
4	I've seen the light; it's the start of a new life.	Realisation

Conclusion: Taking early retirement will not be the end; it will be the beginning of a new adventure.

Step 7: The Merged Dream

There's an alleyway running up the side of my house. Where I live, we call it a ginnel. It's where I used to play as a child, playing hop scotch on the cobbles. You don't see many cobbles these days. They've mostly been taken up and used to build new things. But these cobbles are still here. Same as they always were. Unchanged. Enduring.

Inside, my house is a bit of a mess. Unusual for me. I've always been so particular about keeping my home clean and tidy and nicely decorated. I pick at the peeling paint on the stair banister. I never realised how beautiful the wood underneath was. Glancing round, I see signs of deterioration everywhere. I wander into the kitchen. What a mess! Clutter everywhere. But then, I'm disabled you know. I've had a hip operation and I'm still limping. At least, I think that's what happened to me. Strange that I don't remember having the operation though!

Suddenly, there's a knock at the door and I go to answer it. It's a woman who seems to know me. I don't recognise her but she seems nice so I let her in. Oh my, she's waved her hand across my kitchen and all the clutter has miraculously vanished! How can that be? Truly awesome! She turns to me and, with a compassionate smile, gestures toward the leg that's giving me so many problems,

"Why do you carry this disability around with you? Why do you choose to limp when you can run and skip?" I don't know how to answer her. I thought my disability was real. She asks me the date of my appointment. What appointment? I don't know what she's talking about. She smiles a wise smile. Ah yes, my appointment with the Grim Reaper. Now I understand.

After she has left, I grab my coat and head for the theatre where I do my amateur dramatics. There's a rehearsal and I'm late. I notice that I'm not limping any more. As I wait in the wings for my cue, a girl, whose head is full of writing, approaches and puts her face up close to mine. She's so close; I can feel her breath on my cheek.

"Fate might give you a new role to play," she breathes the words like they have been blown in by the sea, "See the man over there, in the shadows? He's a casting Director and he's watching you." Suddenly, the footlights are switched on, illuminating the whole stage. Then more lights come on, even brighter, filling my eyes with the light of understanding. I can feel the excitement bubbling inside me. No need to be afraid. The light brings new opportunities and new adventures. There's no more need for resistance. There are no enemies left to fight. The light is inviting me onto the stage.

Step 8: Action

These are the action points that the dream series suggested to me. It's a good idea to review the dreams and your Action List from time to time; you may find more ideas spring to mind.

1. Apply for early retirement and commit at least six months to writing.

2. Clear my clutter – a cluttered environment = cluttered thought processes

3. Peel away all the superfluous personas I've used over the years to mask my inadequacies, (yes, we all do it!) Get back to the "bare wood" and apply a fresh coat of paint.

4. Recognise that I have a subconscious resistance to being a successful writer, stemming from the belief of my inner child that I can never achieve this dream because of subjugation, disempowerment and victimization, (all aspects believed by me to be embodied within the concept of a Jewish person). I ask the reader to understand that this is not a reflection on my up-bringing, it's just how the child that I was, interpreted the world I grew up in, for whatever reason. This belief has affected many areas of my life and is still a work in progress.

5. Accept that there is a part of me that is enduring and unchanging – the part that has always wanted to be a writer.

6. Explore more fully the image of the alley way in Dream 1. It was an important part of mine, and my siblings, childhood environment. It not only provided access to the rear of the house, but was also a play area for us. I will ask my siblings for their memories associated with this area.

7. I may consider taking a formal course to improve my writing.

8. Perhaps I could consider writing a play for a local amateur dramatic group, or perhaps something for radio or television.

9. By way of earning money, I could consider giving guest lectures at Universities.

10. I could write articles for magazines

You may remember me saying earlier that it's important to watch out for further dreams that are related to the same issue, following analysis of a dream series. In doing this you can monitor how the messages change over time. It is, therefore, fitting that I end this section with a couple of dreams that occurred after the decision to take early retirement had been made. The first dream occurred four weeks later and the second, three months later. Why don't you use the method described in "session 3, exercise 4; If this were my dream...." and decide what you think these dreams would mean if you'd been the dreamer.

Dream Title: *Follow the white orb*

I'm at the top of the alley way at the side of my childhood home, (the same alley way as in Dream 1). I'm trying to catch hold of a small, white orb that is about the size of a ping pong ball. Every time I get near it, and try to grab it, it moves away. It goes down the alley way, across the road and down another alley way. I follow it. I have the impression that it's leading me to something; something it wants to show me.

Dream Title: *Clearing the clutter*

I'm in the kitchen of my childhood home. I've just cleaned all the cupboards out. There's lots of food on the counters and I'm putting it away into the cupboards. My Mum and sister are here with me. My sister is telling Mum about a new sort of food that makes you lose weight providing you stick to the manufacturer's recommendations. It was a nice dream.

I hope you've found this session interesting, and have found it useful to read how I've approached my own dreams. Remember, we are all unique, all different, and you may have your own ideas about some of the conclusions I've come to. But remember the golden rule; only the dreamer can accurately know what their dreams are telling them. You'll know when you've hit on the meaning of your own dreams because you'll experience the same "Aha" or "Wow" factor that my Dream Ego experienced when she saw the lights in the lecture theatre.

Good luck with discovering your own grand plan. The last session will look at how you can make your grand plan a reality.

Notes

Session 7:
Bringing it all together

"Life is full of beauty. Notice it. Notice the bumble bee, the small child, and the smiling faces. Smell the rain, and feel the wind. Live your life to the fullest potential, and fight for your dreams." Ashley Smith

Session 7:
Bringing it all together

7.1 The final push

I'm hoping you've completed all the exercises before arriving here at the last session in the book. If so, you should now be ready for the final push. I've shown you some of the techniques and tools that you can use to develop your dreaming skills. You've had the opportunity to incubate dreams and work through them in order to understand their messages. You should now have a much better understanding of yourself, even if it's only in one small area of your life. That's quite an achievement. Freud's royal road to the unconscious is an unending highway that stretches on towards infinity but, by working through this book, you can at least claim to have set out on the journey. You may have met a few obstacles along the way. Some you may have overcome as you went along, others you may have to return to at a later date. This is the joy of working with your dreams; there's always something new to learn about yourself and new challenges rising up to greet you.

Before we embark on our very last exercise, I want you to go back to the dream you recorded for Exercise 1 and interpret it again in light of your new knowledge. See if your interpretation has changed and if so, in what way? What aspects are you considering now that you didn't consider before? Are there any lessons from this dream that you can bring into your life right now? Do you need more information? If so, why not put some questions to your subconscious in the form of incubation?

148

However, we're not finished yet. Remember what I said about buying a road map and not setting foot outside your door? If the skills you've learned so far are to be of any use, you need to take **action**. Without action, your dreams are just curiosities and their messages like unread letters.

So, let's embark on our final task; perhaps the most important one in the whole book. Look again at all the things you came up with in exercises 5 and 6. Review the insights you developed during the in depth analyses in exercises 7 and 9. Now go back to exercise 8 and decide whether what you decided you wanted is still the thing you want more than anything else. Does what you learned in the dream series analysis support you in this? If it does, you can use the list of possible actions that you came up with at the end of Exercise 9. If your goal has changed, for whatever reason, repeat session 6 until you have a list of possible actions you could take to achieve whatever goal you've set yourself. In the space below, write out a statement that describes your overall goal, (e.g. I want to be a more loving person, I want to improve the relationship with my mother, I want to be a writer).

How will you go about achieving this goal? Where will you start? The first step is to make a commitment to yourself that you will at least try. When you do this, something amazing happens; the Universe moves to support you in ways you could never have planned for. Maybe you get a phone call out of the blue, you have a small win on the lottery or someone says something that sets you off on a whole new line of thought. In my own case, the analyses of the dreams used as an example in exercise 9 provided me with the courage to apply for early retirement so that I could spend more time writing. Within four weeks of that decision being made, I was approached by a publisher to write a book and had an article accepted for publication in a professional magazine. That's the magic of commitment birthed from your dreams.

"Until one is committed, there is hesitancy, the chance to draw back, always ineffectiveness. Concerning all acts of initiative (and creation), there is one elementary truth, the ignorance of which kills countless ideas and splendid plans.
The moment one definitely commits oneself and then providence moves too. All sorts of things occur to help one that would never otherwise have occurred. A whole stream of events issues from the decision, raising in one's favour all manner of unforeseen incidents and meetings and material assistance, which no man could have dreamed would have come his way. Whatever you can do, or dream you can, begin it. Boldness has genius, power and magic in it. Begin it now." - Johann Wolfgang Von Goethe

Stick this quote up on your wall, somewhere where you'll see it every day. It will remind you that anything is possible once you commit.

> **Exercise 10 Writing an action plan for change.**
>
> Take your Action Points from Exercise 9: Step 8 and choose just one, one that you think will be challenging, but that you would really love to achieve.

What steps will you need to take to achieve this goal? What will you need to do first? Don't try and swallow the elephant whole. It's much easier to eat him in bite-sized chunks! So start by chopping him into manageable pieces. Break the action point down into smaller steps and then break each step down into its component parts. For instance, if your overall goal is to be a writer, one of your Action Points may be to write, and publish, a travel article about a particular country. Perhaps you know someone who lived in that country for a while; someone who would be good to interview. Firstly, you would need to contact them to find out if, and when, they're willing to talk to you. You'll need to plan what sort of questions you'll ask, and it may, therefore, be prudent to do some research first, perhaps on the internet or in local libraries. Breaking it down into manageable steps like this will make you feel you're progressing day by day.

Every step will take you one step nearer to your goal. People have achieved the impossible with this frame of mind. One small step today, another tomorrow, two steps next week, and then suddenly you turn round and find you're almost there.

Map out all the steps you envisage having to take and put them into a timeline. Don't be afraid to make changes to this plan, or the timeline, should the need arise. Plans should be flexible. Think of yourself as an airline pilot. A plane never flies in a straight line towards its destination. There are all sorts of things happening to knock the plane off course; head winds, tail winds, rain, thunder storms that need to be avoided. The pilot has to keep checking his flight path and correcting his course. This is what you'll have to do on your journey; so constantly monitor your progress and re-adjust your path accordingly. Be prepared for this. Don't be disheartened by it. And don't procrastinate! Schedule a few treats into this time plan. Reaching a milestone is a good time to celebrate with a special treat like a shopping trip, tickets for the theatre, a box of chocolates or a bottle of your favourite wine. Make sure the treats are things you wouldn't otherwise partake of, this will make it all the more special. Why not colour code them on your action plan, so that every time you tick off another task, you'll see your treat is that bit closer? The table below suggests the form your action plan might take; please feel free to adapt it to your own needs.

Example action plan

Overall goal: To be a writer.
Action Point, (lesser goal): to write, and publish, a travel article.

Action	Steps	To be finished by: (date)	Notes	Date finished
Research Asia – geography & culture	Go to local library	6 March	Open 9am – 4pm	6 March
	Travel agents	7 March	There are four on the High Street, two in Market Place	9 March
	Internet research	12 March	Google, Wikipedia	11 March
Interview Mary about her Asian experience	Ring Mary and set up a meeting	6 March	Mary's telephone no. is -	4 March
	Buy a Dictaphone	12 March	On offer at Record Ltd £30	8 March
	Write questions to ask Mary	13 March	Use research as basis for informed questions	15 March
	Interview Mary	16 March	2pm 5, Guru Place, Uptown.	16 March
Treat	**Box of chocolates**			
Write the article	Draw up framework plan	17 March	Outline – most salient points	
	First draft	25 March	Rough draft	
	Second draft	2 April	Refine	
	Edit	10 April	Jane has offered to copy edit	
Publish article	Convert to publishing format	12 April	Publisher requires pdf format	
	Submit / upload	12 April	YME Publishing, 1 Paper Close	
Treat	**A fun day out**			

May I add a word of warning? Very few things in life are gained without some sort of cost, and the journey towards your goal will be no exception. Whether it's your time, your money or something far more important, you can be certain that other things in your life will be affected. Where a major life change is being contemplated, bear in mind that your aeroplane may not get off the ground if the hold is overloaded with baggage. Heavy emotional cargo may need to be left behind or jettisoned. Providing you're still recording your dreams, and taking the time to understand the message contained in them, you will know whether the sacrifices you are contemplating are wise, or even necessary; whether you're heading in the right direction or whether you've veered so far off course that you need a major review of your plan. If by chance, what you're considering, is something that your core self warns you not to do, you can be confident that your dreams will let you know and give you warning of this. So, during all the time you're taking those small steps towards achieving your goal, it's imperative that you continue to record your dreams.

7.2 Take action

After you've written your action plan, all that remains is for you to just go and do it. When you've achieved that first goal, go back to your Action Points in Exercise 9 and choose another goal to start work on. If you're feeling particularly ambitious, you could even work on more than one goal at a time. And keep an open mind; don't be too rigid about sticking to your original intentions. It's likely that other things will occur to you on your journey to achieving your first goal, maybe from an encounter or perhaps another dream; roll with it. Trust your core self, trust your intuition, trust your dreams. And take with you my best wishes for all the success you desire and deserve, and a very happy and productive dreamtime.

May light and love brighten all of your dreams.

END

Further Reading

History of Dreaming

Van de Castle, Robert. (1996) Our Dreaming Mind.
ISBN 0-345-39666-9
Garfield, Patricia (2001) The Universal Dream Key: The 12 Most
Common Dream Themes Around The World.
Harperperennial Library, ISBN: 978-0060953645

Language of Dreams

Fromm, Erich (1952) The Forgotten Language; An Introduction to
the Understanding of Dreams, Fairy Tales, and Myths.
ISBN: 978-0030184369
Jung, Carl. (1990 edn) Man and His Symbols.
ISBN: 978-0140193169

Lucid Dreaming

Laberge, Stephen and Rheingold, Howard (1997) Exploring the
World of Lucid Dreaming. ISBN: 978-0345420121
Waggoner, Robert. (2008) Lucid Dreaming. Gateway to the Inner
Self. ISBN: 978-1930491144

Shamanic Dreaming

Castaneda, Carlos (1993) The Art of Dreaming
ISBN 1-85538-427-2
Moss, Robert. (1996) Conscious Dreaming, A Spiritual Path for
Everyday Life ISBN 0-517-88710-X
Moss, Robert. (2009) The Three Only Things. Tapping the Power
of Dreams, Coincidence and Imagination. ISBN 978-1577316633
Villoldo, Alberto. (2008) Courageous Dreaming. How Shamans
Dream the World into being. ISBN 978-1-4019-1757-9

Working with Dreams

Dee, Nerys (2000) Understanding Dreams: What they are and
how to interpret them. ISBN: 978-0007102761
Crisp ,Tony (2002) Dream Dictionary: An A to Z Guide to
understanding your unconscious mind. ISBN 0-440-23707-6
Harthan, Joan. (2005) Working the Nightshift, How to
understand your dreams. ISBN 1-412-05546-6
Harthan, Ernest (2001) Dreams & Nightmares: the origin and
meaning of dreams. ISBN 0-7382-0359-9

Jung, Carl G. (1991) The Archetypes and the Collective Unconscious (Collected Works of C.G. Jung)
ISBN: 978-0415058445
Krippner, Stanley and Waldman, Mark. (1999) Dreamscaping; New & creative ways to work with your Dreams.
ISBN: 978-0737302684
Ullman, M & Zimmerman, N. (1987) "Working with Dreams."
ISBN: 978-0440392828

Web resources

www.docdreamuk.com
Author's website. Contains interesting information on sleep and dreams, and has useful links to other resources.

www.asdreams.org
Website of the International Association for the Study of Dreams, a non-profit, international, multidisciplinary organisation dedicated to the pure and applied investigation of dreams and dreaming. Their aim is to promote an awareness and appreciation of dreams in both professional and public arenas; to encourage research into the nature, function, and significance of dreaming; to advance the application of the study of dreams; and to provide a forum for the eclectic and interdisciplinary exchange of ideas and information.

http://dreamstudies.org
Website of Ryan Hurd. A scholarly website covering dreaming, culture & consciousness with a web blog that aims to keep visitors updated with current advances in dream work.

http://www.improverse.com/ed-articles/search.htm
Bulging with fascinating and thought-provoking articles from past issues of Electric Dreams 1994 - 2006. All free to access and download.

www.mossdreams.com
Robert Moss, Way of the Dreamer. A website dedicated to Shamanic dreaming.

Please note external references are provided in good faith and we have no control over their content.

Universe of Learning Books

"The purpose of learning is growth, and our minds, unlike our bodies, can continue growing as we continue to live." Mortimer Adler

About the publishers

Universe of Learning Limited is a small publisher based in the UK with production in England and America. Our authors are all experienced trainers or teachers who have taught their skills for many years. We are actively seeking qualified authors and if you visit the authors section on www.uolearn.com you can find out how to apply.

If you are interested in any of our current authors (including Joan Harthan) coming to speak at your event please do visit their own websites (to contact Joan please email joan@uolearn. com or visit www.docdreamuk.com) or email them through the author section of the uolearn site.

If you would like to purchase larger numbers of books then please do contact us (sales@uolearn.com). We give discounts from 5 books upwards. For larger volumes we can also quote for changes to the cover to accommodate your company logo and to the interior to brand it for your company.

All our books are written by teachers, trainers or people well experienced in their roles and our goal is to help people develop their skills with a well structured range of exercises.

If you have any feedback about this book or other topics that you'd like to see us cover please do contact us at support@uolearn.com.

To buy the printed books please order from your favourite bookshop, including Amazon, Waterstones, Blackwells and Barnes and Noble. For ebooks please visit www.uolearn.com.

Keep Learning!

Speed Writing

Speedwriting for faster note taking and dictation

ISBN 978-1-84937-011-0, from www.uolearn.com

Easy exercises to learn faster writing in just 6 hours.

- ✓ "The principles are very easy to follow, and I am already using it to take notes."
- ✓ "I will use this system all the time."
- ✓ "Your system is so easy to learn and use."

Report Writing

An easy to follow format for writing reports

ISBN 978-1-84937-036-3, from www.uolearn.com

This book makes report writing a step by step process for you to follow every time you have a report to write.

- ✓ How to set objectives using 8 simple questions
- ✓ Easy to follow flow chart
- ✓ How to write an executive summary
- ✓ How to layout and structure the report
- ✓ Help people remember what they read

Speed Reading
Skills Training Course

How to read a book, report or short document on paper or online three times as fast with comprehension for study skills and business

ISBN: 978-1-84937-021-9, Order at www.uolearn.com

Would you like to learn simple techniques to help you read 3 times as fast?

This book has a series of easy to follow guided exercises that help you change your reading habits to both read faster and to evaluate which parts to read and in what order.

Study Skills Training Course

How to pass your exam, test or coursework easily

Improve your learning skills to pass exams and assessments, take notes, memorize facts and speed read, for studying at school and college

ISBN: 978-1-84937-020-2, Order at www.uolearn.com

Dr Greenhall's techniques helped her to get a first class honours degree in physics and chemistry, a doctorate in science and an MA in education, easily and with little effort. Guided exercises will help you to learn the secrets of these successes.

How to Start a Business as a Private Tutor

ISBN 978-1-84937-029-5, from www.uolearn.com

This book, by a Lancashire based author, shows you how to set up your own business as a tutor.

✓ Packed with tips and stories
✓ How to get started - what to do and buy
✓ How to attract clients and advertise
✓ Free printable forms, ready to use
✓ Advice on preparing students for exams

Successful Minute Taking Meeting the Challenge

How to prepare, write and organise agendas and minutes of meetings

ISBN 978-1-84937-040-0, from www.uolearn.com

✓ Becoming more confident in your role
✓ A checklist of what to do
✓ Help with layout and writing skills
✓ Learn what to include in minutes
✓ How to work well with your chairperson

Learn to be an excellent meeting secretary.

Coaching Skills Training Course

Business and life coaching techniques for

ISBN: 978-1-84937-019-6, from www.uolearn.com
- ✓ An easy to follow 5 step model
- ✓ Learn to both self-coach and coach others
- ✓ Over 25 ready to use ideas
- ✓ Goal setting tools to help achieve ambitions

A toolbox of ideas to help you become a great coach

Stress Management

Exercises and techniques to manage stress and anxiety

ISBN: 978-1-84937-002-8, from www.uolearn.com
- ✓ Understand what stress is
- ✓ Become proactive in managing your stress
- ✓ Learn how to change your response to stress
- ✓ How to become more positive about your life
- ✓ An easy 4 step model to lasting change

Practical and Effective Performance Management

ISBN: 978-1-84937-037-0, from www.uolearn.com
- ✓ Five key ideas to understanding performance
- ✓ A clear four step model
- ✓ Key what works research that is practical
- ✓ A large, wide ranging choice of tools
- ✓ Practical exercises and action planning for managers.
  A toolbox of ideas to help you become a better leader.

Developing Your Influencing Skills

ISBN: 978-1-84937-004-2, from www.uolearn.com
- ✓ Decide what your influencing goals are
- ✓ Find ways to increase your credibility rating
- ✓ Develop stronger and more trusting relationships
- ✓ Inspire others to follow your lead
- ✓ Become a more influential communicator

Packed with case studies, exercises and practical tips to become more influential.

"Make your life a work of art.
Your dreams are your paints,
the world is your canvas.
Believing, is the brush that converts your
dreams into a masterpiece of reality."

Lightning Source UK Ltd.
Milton Keynes UK
UKOW020426210513

210983UK00003B/69/P